Vegetarian Food for All

Vegetarian Food for All

Zesty International Dishes from One of the
World's Most Celebrated Natural Foods
Restaurants

by Annabel Perkins

New World Library
Novato, California

New World Library
14 Pamaron Way
Novato, California 94949

Cover Design by Michael McClure
Illustrations by Albert Perkins,
Grethe Swahn-Zibell, and Michael McClure
Text design by Aaron Kenedi

Library of Congress Cataloging-in-Publication Data

Perkins, Annabel, 1957
Vegetarian Food for All : Zesty international dishes from one of the world's
most celebrated natural foods restaurants / by
Annabel Perkins
p.   cm.
ISBN 0-945934-13-0 (alk. paper)
1. Cookery, Vegetarian. 2. Food for All (Restaurant) I. Title
TX837.P48
641.5'636 — dc20   95-36482 CIP

First printing, May 1996
Printed in the U.S.A. on acid-free paper
ISBN 0-945934-13-0
Distributed to the trade by Publishers Group West

Table of Contents

Introduction

The original manuscript for this book was written in England in 1977 when I was expecting my first child. I had the honor of writing it in the very room used by Nicholas Monsarrat when he was writing his famous war novel, *The Cruel Sea*. Later my son was born in this same room. At the time of writing the book (my book!) the huge old house belonged to a yoga community of which I was a member. We had recently opened Food for All, a vegetarian restaurant, whole food store, bakery, and community printing press all in one. Those early days were full of excitement, tears, and grindingly hard work. A typical day began at 5 A.M. with a visit to the local farmers' market where we bought all our fresh fruits, vegetables, and cheeses. Some days one or two items would be exceptionally cheap and plentiful, so we would haggle the prices down to rock-bottom and return laden with crates of such humble items as rutabagas, red cabbages, and Jerusalem artichokes. Many of our recipes were invented to utilize these plain vegetables in creative ways to cook inexpensive, tasty meals that nourished our faithful clientele — a mixture of students, gentle elderly vegetarian couples, and the avant-garde who inhabited the gracefully decaying Victorian mansions of the old part of the city, near the restaurant.

At 9 A.M., after a short breakfast, we would drive to the restaurant kitchen, and there would follow three hours of frantic cooking and salad preparation. It was during these mornings of hectic work that I was taught to cook by a friend and fellow yoga student, Triipti Drake-Law. She always amazed me with her versatility and ingenuity in using only simple techniques and ingredients to create delicious, balanced meals. From such meals grew this cookbook.

From noon until 2 P.M. we would dash around serving the food, making tea and coffee, and clearing the tables. We made good friends with many of our customers who became inveterate regulars. Then, after a short rest in which we gorged ourselves on all the delicious stuff we had been watching other people getting their teeth into, we would do the whole thing again in the afternoon, for the evening session. After closing at 9 P.M. we scoured the kitchen from end to end until midnight.

The restaurant became a big success, and people began to ask for the recipes. Many of our customers had never eaten vegetarian food before, and scarcely knew what the ingredients were. The need for a basic cookbook became apparent. When I became pregnant, I was no longer able to lift the heavy pots of soup for fifty people, so we decided that I should instead write the book. Following the principles with which the restaurant had been so successful, my aim is to bring you simple, inexpensive, nutritious food, creatively prepared in the spirit of the yoga philosophy.

Consequently, there is little haute cuisine in this book. The recipes are fast and simple enough to be sustainably cookable from day to day, flexible enough to change with the seasons and to allow for your own tastes and creativity. My goal is to suggest ideas and techniques which you can adapt to your own tastes and needs to such an extent that the cookbook will come to be unnecessary. I hope that, like me, you will experiment liberally with a wide variety of herbs and spices and gain the confidence to move away from the inevitable onion and garlic that swamp every subtle flavor in Western vegetarian food. I hope, too, that you will enjoy simply throwing whatever seems to be yummy into a pot and creating something entirely new. There is literally infinite potential for this. There are so many different ways you can combine ingredients — you really can create something new every day.

The first edition (6,000 copies) of the book was published in the fall of 1977. It sold out in three months, and our ambitious plans to revise and republish were never realized. But finally, here it is again, with all the old favorites and lots of new ones too, the fruits of much fun and hard work cooking, eating, and digesting.

In addition to Triipti's input, without which I am sure this book could never have been written, I would like to thank Arete and Scott Brim for their generous help and support inputting the manuscript, Jyoti Bailey for comradeship, inspiration, and many, many recipe ideas (the first time I tasted her cooking I couldn't believe that anybody could cook like this), my husband Amal, who published the first book and ate the food so enthusiastically, and many friends who generously contributed their own recipes and retested some of the originals.

I dedicate this book to all who struggle to realize a new era of peace and harmony on the earth, both internally in their own souls, and externally through their united efforts to create a better universal society of people, animals, and plants.

Vegetarianism

This is a vegetarian cookbook, and the chances are that you, the cook, are vegan or vegetarian already. If not, you may ask what good reasons there are for becoming vegetarian.

The cruelty issue is perhaps the most obvious, and with the advent of factory farming, conditions for domestic animals are worse than ever before. Some people try to get around this problem by buying free-range produce, but it may still be asked whether we have the authority to destroy life that we have no power to create.

Meat is costly to produce, relative to other foods, for two reasons. First, high proportions of valuable foodstuffs are exported each year by developing countries to meet debt repayment commitments, or simply because the developed countries can afford to pay higher prices. Thus, food fit for human consumption and acutely needed by hungry people in developing countries is fed to the cattle of the developed world, who only yield back a fraction in the form of meat. If you haven't already done so, read *Diet for a Small Planet* by Frances Moore Lappé which gives realistic information about the so-called world food crisis and how the economic issues can be resolved to solve this disgraceful problem. Meanwhile, you as consumer, in refusing to buy meat products, are taking a significant step in the direction of eliminating world hunger.

The second reason meat is so costly is because its production is devastating to the environment. Meat production is responsible for the loss of ancient forests to ranch land, soil erosion by overgrazing, and water contamination due to animal waste. The meat industry consumes vast quantities of fresh water. The problem of water shortage is becoming more acute every year and the quest for new sources itself causes environmental devastation.

Finally, consider the detrimental effects of meat consumption on human health. Excessive animal fat and protein intake is linked to heart disease, cancer, strokes, arthritis, and other chronic diseases of the developed world. Additionally, factory-farmed meat is contaminated with pesticides, antibiotic and hormone residues, dyes, and preservatives. Chickens are routinely fed their own excrement, while cows, naturally vegetarian animals, are often fed the entrails of slaughtered animals. The old adage "You are what you eat" applies to them as well as to us.

For more information on the health and environmental consequenses of consuming animal foods, and the factory farming industry, see *Diet for a New America*, by John Robbins.

Meat-eating has also been linked to aggressive behavior in animals and human beings alike, and this is one reason why meat has been rejected by practitioners of yoga for 7,000 years.

Note for Vegans: Most of the recipes in this book adapt well to vegan substitutes for butter, milk, and cream. For optimal flavor, use rice-based substitutes in recipes calling for milk.

Food and Yoga

You will notice that the recipes in this book contain no eggs, onions, garlic, leeks, or mushrooms. Refined and canned foods are also mostly avoided, and instead the use of whole food is preferred. Wholeness preserves health. Foods direct from the earth, with the minimum of processing are the most complete, the most wholesome. They nourish our bodies and minds.

What is the Nourishment of the Mind?

The practice of yoga is the search for oneness, for wholeness, a feeling of unity with the divinity within the self. According to yoga philosophy there are three basic kinds of energy or binding principles which influence us. The most dominant principle is the static force, with the attributes of inertia, death, and decay. The foods dominated by this static force are those that are spoiled; dead flesh (meat); irritating foods (onions and garlic—these foods have a slightly irritating effect on the body, which also affects one's mental state); and meat-like foods (fish, poultry, eggs, and mushrooms.) "It is not yet determined whether fungi are animals or vegetables. They have all the properties of animal foods and must be considered as such," says Dr. Robinson, the 19th century American herbalist. Yoga practitioners of ancient India knew about these meat-like properties of mushrooms, and therefore avoided eating them. Alcohol, tobacco, and so-called recreational drugs are definitely harmful to the body and belong to the static category.

The second binding principle, less dominant than the static, is the mutative force. Its characteristic is change and movement, and stimulation. Therefore stimulating foods such as tea, coffee, and cocoa fall into this category. These foods have an unsettling effect on body and mind and may be harmful when taken to excess.

The third binding principle is the sentient force, which is in direct contrast to the static, inert energy force. Its attributes are life, growth, and progressive expansion on both the physical and psychic levels. Foods which fall into this category might be called foods of intuition. They promote the harmonious balance of the mind and aid in concentration. Since the body is constantly regenerating cells, those cells built out of sentient foodstuffs are of a finer or subtler nature than cells produced by a mutative or static diet. Therefore one's mind and body become a subtler vehicle for mental expansion and spiritual realization. What are these wonderful foods? Krishna (a great Indian saint) said, ". . . those foods which are sweet, juicy and delicious, fresh fruit and vegetables and their juices, dairy products, nuts, honey and cereals."

> *"Out of Brahman, who is self, came Akasha; out of Akasha, air; out of air, fire; out of fire, water; out of water, earth; out of earth, vegetation; out of vegetation, food; out of food the body of man. The body of man, composed of food, is the physical sheath of the Self.*
> *"From food are born all creatures, which live upon food, and after death return to food. Food is the chief of all things. It is therefore said to be the medicine of all diseases of the body. Those who worship food as Brahman gain all material objects. From food are born all things which, being born, grow by food. All beings feed upon food, and, when they die, food feeds on them."*

> — From the Upanishads

Remember always to cook in a clean, relaxed environment, and to treat your materials with respect. Food has its own awareness. Treat it lovingly. It is better to dine in company than to dine alone. Food cooked with love and eaten in an atmosphere of friendship nourishes the body, mind, and spirit.

Chapter 1

Kitchen Equipment

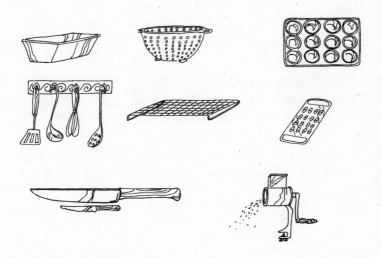

Saucepans

You may already know that aluminum is a poison that we should try to avoid eating. The aluminum from your pots can leach into the food and may contaminate it. Lightweight pots with special finishes are convenient, but can burn easily and may also contaminate the food. The best pans you can buy are made of stainless steel and have copper layers sandwiched into the base, which helps distribute the heat evenly. These pots are light to carry and nothing burns or sticks easily. They are usually expensive, but if cared for will last a lifetime.

Enameled cast iron pots look beautiful and cook gently, but are heavy to carry, and if dropped they may crack and be permanently damaged. The enamel will also chip and wear away. These pots are also expensive. For a low-cost alternative to aluminum, consider glassware or unenamelled cast iron. A double boiler saucepan is composed of two separate saucepans, one fitting inside the other. Water is kept at a boil in the pan underneath and cooks the food, which is placed in the top pan. This means that the food is cooked very slowly over indirect heat, a very good method when very long, slow, gentle cooking is required, e.g. some sauces, foods that easily burn, and very delicate foods.

An arrangement for steaming vegetables is easy to make. A wire rack or enamel colander that fits inside a pan is enough.

A pressure cooker is very convenient for cooking beans that would otherwise take hours, and cooking vegetables in only a few minutes.

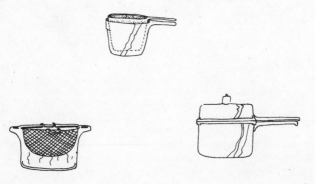

Frying Pans

A skillet is a large, deep flat-bottomed frying pan. The best ones are made of cast iron — the heavier the better. Used for dry roasting, frying, sautéing, and can also be used to make stews and curries. An ordinary frying pan can be adapted to all these purposes, too.

A wok is a round-bottomed frying pan used in Chinese cooking. The oil collects in the concave bottom and the finely chopped vegetables are tossed in and out of the hot oil and across the scorching surface of the metal. Vegetables are cooked very quickly and retain their goodness and bright color. The wok is ideal for sautéing vegetables, and for making Chinese-style dishes.

A griddle is a flat plate with a handle, for making drop scones, chapatis, pancakes, and the like.

Blender and/or Food Processor

An electric blender or food processor is a good investment, since it makes delicious creamy soups, smooth purees and sauces, milk shakes, and fresh, inexpensive, nutritious baby food. Some electric blenders have a grinding attachment which means that you can grind whole spices freshly as needed, and the taste is sharper. Ground spices kept in jars soon go stale. A food processor will also perform tedious or wrist-breaking jobs like chopping and grating vegetables, kneading dough, and whipping cream. A must for working parents or for the congenitally lazy. A mortar and pestle will also grind spices.

Other Equipment

In addition to those already mentioned, you may want to obtain the following:

- a casserole pan for the oven — pyrex or earthenware
- some loaf tins and baking trays made of tin
- a cooling rack so that cakes, loaves, and cookies won't stay in the tin and go soggy
- a spatula, a soup ladle, a wire whisk, and a slotted ladle
- a grater
- a colander
- one or two sharp knives for chopping vegetables
- a food grinder or mincer for nuts, bread crumbs, cheese, patés, etc.

Recycling

There's a lot of trash floating around nowadays. We don't know what to do with it all any longer. Try to buy food with the minimum of packaging. A lot of packaging means that the food has been subjected to more factory processing. Recycle as much as you can, and consider buying food in bulk cooperatively with friends and neighbors. You save money this way too.

Organic refuse rots and turns into good-quality fertilizing compost. If you don't have a garden to feed, a neighbor would probably welcome your organic waste.

Quantities Used in Recipes

1 American pt = 500 ml

1 oz = 28 $^1/_2$ g

2 oz = 57 g

4 oz = 114 g

8 oz = 227 g

1 lb = 454 g

1 T = 1 large, old-fashioned tablespoon (15 mls)

1 t = 1 teaspoon (5 mls)

1 C = 1 cup (8 fluid ounces)

Chapter 2

Oils, Grains, and Pasta

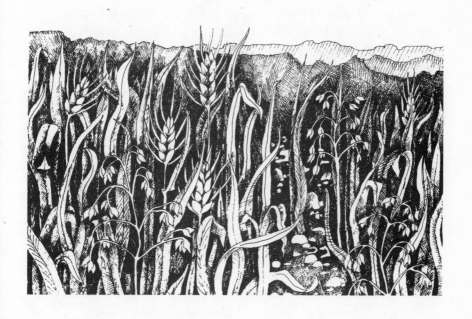

Oils

When choosing oil for cooking, it is wise to consider the way in which it has been extracted from the oil seed. The most expensive oils are cold-pressed; that is, the oil is extracted from the seed by pressure alone. This kind of oil contains all the nutrients present in the original seed in an unprocessed and wholesome form, and the oil retains the characteristic smell and flavor of the original seed. This is an expensive method of extraction, because it does not remove all the oil from the seed. Oils prepared in this way are by far the most wholesome, though. The vitamin E naturally present prevents the oil from becoming rancid, but not for long. The oil should be used as fresh as possible and always stored in the refrigerator in a covered container.

Another method of extraction uses a screw, or continuous press. The seed is first cooked and then squeezed under continuous pressure until discharged at the other end of the machine with the oil squeezed out. Because it is necessary to cook the seed to increase the proportion of oil extracted, the oil has a strong smell and dark color which makes refining necessary. The heat and refining used in this process therefore destroys the vitamins and renders the oil flavorless. Antioxidants are also often added to replace the oil's natural preservative, vitamin E, which is lost in the extraction process.

Solvent extraction is the most efficient method and also gives the highest extraction rate, so it is very popular with oil refiners. It is also dangerous to our health. The oil seeds are ground, cooked, and then mixed with the solvents that dissolve out the oil, leaving a dry residue. The solvent is usually petroleum-based. The resulting mixture is then heated, passed through caustic soda, bleached with Fuller's Earth®, and finally deodorized by having steam passed through it under vacuum. This oil is not only empty of vitamins and flavor, but always contains traces of the petroleum solvents used, which are cancer-producing. This is the oil from which margarine is usually made.

Unsaturated oils are those that contain long chains of carbon atoms with vacant spaces which are easily filled by other atoms. For example when the vacant spaces are filled with oxygen, rancidity occurs, a process that takes place very rapidly when the oil is heated. Rancid oil is unhealthy. The oxygen will readily leave the carbon chains and join other molecules in the body, such as vitamins, oxidizing or burning them and changing their structure so that they are no longer useful to the body. For this reason, left-over oil which has been used for deep-frying should not be re-used. It is also wise to avoid using margarine. Solid margarine is typically made with animal fat, while the more expensive margarine is manufactured from vegetable oil that has had hydrogen gas passed through it. In this case it is the hydrogen that fills the vacant spaces along the carbon chains, and causes the oil to saturate and solidify (rather than go rancid). Contrary to the belief of a few years ago, there is increasing evidence to suggest that hydrogenated oils actually contribute to heart disease, and that it is, in fact, healthier to use butter! To quote Rudolf Ballantine, M.D., (*Diet and Nutrition: A Wholistic Approach*, 1989, Himalayan International Institute), "There is some data suggesting that butter fat, unlike other animal fats, actually has a protective effect on the heart." Ballantine comes down in favor of butter even over unsaturated oils because of their tendency to oxidize so rapidly. Obviously the debate over unsaturated versus saturated fat will continue. Meanwhile, a tasty alternative to pure butter, for the unconvinced, may be made by blending melted butter with olive oil in equal proportions. This will solidify in the refrigerator and keeps well.

Unless otherwise stated, I have used fresh cold-pressed canola oil, or olive oil, whenever oil is called for in the recipes.

Whole Grains and Pastas

Whole grains are very important to vegetarians since they contain both the seed and fruit of the plant, and thus contribute all the essential elements needed for a new cycle of life for the plant. Grains are best eaten in their whole state, with all their vital life force intact, but are also often eaten flaked or ground, in which case they should be very fresh.

Rice

Brown rice contains 25% more protein than white rice, is richer in vitamins of the B group, and contains the minerals calcium, iron, and phosphorus. It is a less concentrated starch than white rice because of its high fiber content. There are two basic types of brown rice, long and short grain. The long-grain tends to be crisper and more fluffy, so it is better for eating alone, or with savory dishes, whereas short-grain rice is better used in puddings.

HOW TO COOK BROWN RICE:
Serves 3-4

1 C RICE
2 ¹/₂ C WATER
PINCH OF SALT

Salt the water and bring it to a boil. Wash the rice and add it so slowly that the water never stops boiling. Stir once, lower the heat and simmer 30 to 40 minutes until the grain is tender.

Do not stir any more! As the rice expands, it forms a network of steam tunnels. If these are disturbed, the grains will cook unevenly, with the bottom soggy or burned, and the top not done. Remove the pot from the heat 5 minutes before the end of cooking. The job is then finished by the heat inside, and you avoid a burnt pot. To give different flavors to the rice, you could try sautéing it in butter with your favorite herbs before adding it to the water.

YOU COULD TRY ADDING A FEW MORE INGREDIENTS TO THE FRITTER MIXTURE. TRY SOME OF THESE:

CHOPPED PARSLEY, SAUTÉED CELERY AND WALNUTS
FRESH TOMATOES, CHOPPED, AND BASIL
CINNAMON AND PAPRIKA
LEFTOVER BEANS OR COOKED VEGETABLES, WITH HERBS, FOR EXAMPLE, A LITTLE THYME, MARJORAM, SAGE, OR MINT.

Rice Fritters

Add a little extra salt and some black pepper to cooked rice. Squeeze a handful of rice tightly into a ball. Now form it into a thick patty and fry in hot oil for 2 to 3 minutes on either side.

Millet

Millet is perhaps the earliest known cereal. Today it is the staple diet of a large part of the world. In India alone 40 million acres are used for its cultivation. Millet is a very light cereal, its texture not unlike mashed potato. When cooked, it swells up to 3 or 4 times its original volume. It is high in protein and easy to digest.

How to Cook Millet:

Serves 2-3

1 C MILLET

1 T OIL (FOR SAUTÉING)

3 C WATER

PINCH OF SALT

Sauté the millet in oil until golden, then add water and salt. Bring to a boil, cover and simmer slowly for 20 to 25 minutes. It should be light and fluffy when cooked. Millet burns easily, so remove the pot from the heat 5 minutes before the end of cooking.

Crispy Millet Balls

Add chunks of freshly-chopped parsley to cooked millet. Roll the mixture into egg-sized balls (the millet sticks together better if cooked without sautéing first) and deep-fry until golden. The oil is hot enough for frying when a small piece of bread dropped into it sizzles and fries in about 10 seconds.

Millet Bake with Cheese and Tomato

Mix a little butter and whole grain mustard into cooked millet. Spread the millet in a shallow baking tray and cover the surface with grated cheese. Decorate the top with rings of tomato, and bake at 350° until crisp on top.

2 ¹/₂ C SPINACH, SHREDDED

3 C WATER, WITH PINCH OF SALT

I C UNCOOKED MILLET

¹/₂ OZ BUTTER OR ¹/₂ T OIL

SALT AND PEPPER

Millet with Spinach

Serves 2

Cook the spinach for a few minutes in salted water. Drain and set it aside. Rinse the millet and cook it in the water left from the spinach. When ready, mix the spinach into the millet with some butter or oil, and a little pepper.

Corn (Maize)

Sweet Corn

To cook corn on the cob, place the cobs into boiling salted water and boil fast until tender. Eat them with butter, salt and pepper. A tidier way of eating fresh sweet corn is to strip it from the cob and then cook it. Fresh sweet corn has a fresher, livelier taste than the canned variety. To strip the cob, cut down the middle of each line of grain with a sharp knife. Now scrape off the grains, from halfway down the cob towards the bottom. Turn it upside down to do the top half. When scraped, the corn can be used as a tasty stuffing for peppers and tomatoes.

Sweet Corn on Toast

Place the corn in a heavy saucepan or double boiler with a pinch of salt and some freshly ground black pepper, a tablespoon of butter and a little milk. Cook very gently for 20 minutes. Serve on hot buttered toast.

Popcorn

Popcorn is made from the popcorn kernels after they have ripened and hardened. To make popcorn, use a big pan with a tight-fitting lid. Drop the kernels into a little very hot oil in the bottom of the pan, and put the lid on quickly. You will hear them exploding inside. Shake the pan regularly. When the popping stops the corn is ready. Sprinkle it with salt, or pour a little honey over it. Don't use too many popcorn kernals, because they grow immensely during cooking, as you will discover.

CORNMEAL

Cornmeal is the flour ground from the grain. In Mexico this is used to make tortillas, which are an essential ingredient in Enchiladas (p. 112). The Italians also use cornmeal to make a traditional dish called polenta.

4 C WATER WITH A PINCH OF SALT
I C YELLOW CORNMEAL
2 OZ ($^1/_2$ STICK) BUTTER
3 TOMATOES PEELED AND CHOPPED
2 T FRESH CHOPPED PARSLEY
I T DRIED BASIL, OR **3** FRESH LEAVES
I C GRATED PARMESAN CHEESE
SALT AND FRESHLY GROUND PEPPER

Polenta
Serves 4

Mix 1½ C of the salted water with the cornmeal in a heavy saucepan. Heat remaining water to boiling and gradually add this mixture. Bring back to a boil, stirring constantly. Add salt to taste, lower heat and cook slowly, stirring regularly, for about 20 minutes. Pour into a buttered casserole dish. In a separate pan, sauté the tomatoes and herbs in the butter for about 10 minutes to make a sauce. Add seasoning and spread this over the cornmeal. Cover with parmesan cheese and bake 10 to 13 minutes at 350° until cheese is well melted. Serve with a green salad.

CORNSTARCH

Cornstarch is a refined starch made from maize which is used as a thickener for blancmange, custards and sauces. It is inexpensive, but because it is refined it cannot be called a whole food. For thickening purposes, you may prefer to use arrowroot.

Buckwheat

Buckwheat is a nutritious and fortifying grain, grown and eaten mainly in Russia, where it is called kasha. Buckwheat is rich in B-group and E vitamins. It also contains a substance called rutin, which strengthens the walls of arteries, and helps reduce high blood pressure. It may be purchased roasted or unroasted. Buckwheat spaghetti is tasty, and can be bought in health food shops.

Buckwheat flour can also be used to make delicious pancakes, using 1 C ordinary whole wheat flour to each C of buckwheat flour. A little buckwheat flour added to a vegetable crumble mix also gives a delicious flavor.

Buckwheat can be eaten with vegetables and sauce. It makes a satisfying breakfast eaten alone or with yogurt and fruit, and it is good with a little honey or tahini. You can also make delicious fritters with it.

How to Cook Buckwheat:
Serves 2-3

1 C BUCKWHEAT

3 C WATER

SALT TO TASTE

1/2 T OIL (FOR SAUTÉING)

Bring the water to a boil and add salt. Heat oil and sauté buckwheat until crisp. Add boiling water to the buckwheat, cover, and remove from heat, leaving the grain to swell. Roasted buckwheat needs no further cooking, but if unroasted it may need to simmer a little.

I **C** ROASTED BUCKWHEAT
3 **C** WATER
I **t** GROUND CORIANDER
¹/₂ **t** CELERY SEED
I **t** SAGE
¹/₂ **t** GALANGAL
I **t** DRY BASIL
I **T** TOMATO PASTE
I **T** TAMARI (SOY SAUCE)
SALT AND PEPPER TO TASTE
UNBLEACHED FLOUR (FOR COATING)
OIL (FOR DEEP FRYING)

Buckwheat Fritters

Makes twelve 2-inch diameter fritters

Place buckwheat and water in a saucepan with a pinch of salt, bring to a boil, then turn down the heat and simmer 2-3 minutes. Set aside to swell for 10-15 minutes. Mix in all other ingredients. Form the mixture into patties by making a ball the size of a large egg and flattening it slightly. Dip in flour and fry in a heavy skillet in 1-inch of hot oil on both sides until crisp on the outside. Place balls on several layers of paper towels to dry.

Rye Grain, Whole Wheat, and Pot Barley

Frugal, simple and nutritious, and eaten only with fresh vegetables, these simple whole grains make a delicious, and clean-tasting meal.

How to Cook Rye:
Serves 2-3

I **C** RYE
3 **C** WATER
I **T** SALT

Rye grain is best soaked overnight before cooking, to make it more digestible. Bring water to a boil, add salt, and simmer the grain for 1 hour, adding more water if necessary. In a pressure cooker, the grain takes about 40 minutes. Use 1 C rye to 1¹/₂ C water. If the rye is not pre-soaked, the cooking time will be longer and ¹/₂ C more water should be added.

Barley

The cultivation of barley goes back to prehistoric times and originates in Syria and Egypt. Pot barley is the whole grain, white pearl barley has had its brown coat removed. Pot barley is therefore better from the nutritional aspect. Barley flakes are good in muesli mix. They should be soaked overnight before eating.

How to Cook Barley:
Serves 3

1 C POT BARLEY OR PEARL BARLEY, SOAKED OVERNIGHT AND DRAINED
4-5 C WATER

Pre-soak the barley. Bring water to a boil and add barley. Cook pot barley 1 to 1 1/2 hours, ensuring it does not simmer dry. Cook pearl barley 45 minutes. Barley should not be cooked in a pressure cooker, as the starch released during cooking will clog the safety valve.

Wheat

Whole wheatberries are very tasty. Soak overnight, drain, then use 1 C wheat to 3 C water. Cook 1 to 1 1/2 hours, adding more water when necessary. The soaking water is rich in enzymes. You can drink it or feed it to your house plants. 1 C wheatberries is enough for 3 to 4 people. In addition to wheatberries, try two coarse grain wheat products available from health food stores: bulgur wheat and couscous. Bulgur is cracked wheat grain that has already been partially cooked and dried. Couscous is lighter than bulgur wheat in color and has a more delicate flavor.

Couscous and bulgur can be used in any way you would use rice. For example, serve as the basis of a vegetarian meal with sauces and vegetables, or use in salads, fritters, and stuffings for vegetables.

How to Cook Couscous:
Serves 2

1 C COUSCOUS
1 T BUTTER
2 ¹/₂ C WATER

Sauté couscous in butter for 1 minute in a heavy saucepan. Add water, bring to a boil, cover and simmer gently without stirring for 10 minutes or until the water is absorbed.

How to Cook Bulgur:
Serves 2-3

1 C BULGUR
2 ¹/₂ C WATER
PINCH OF SALT

Place the bulgur in the cold water, bring to a boil, cover and simmer gently for 10 to 15 minutes.

Pasta

There are many varieties of pasta available. For variety try spinach flavored pasta, vermicelli (a very fine, fast-cooking pasta popular with children) and pasta flavored with artichoke. There is also a type of transparent vermicelli available in Chinese stores, called cellophane noodle (made with bean starch or rice), which can be used in soups as a change from wheat pasta. See the recipe for Mock Duck Noodle Soup (p. 109).

3 C WHEAT PASTA SPIRALS
¹/₂ C SOUR CREAM
¹/₂ t PAPRIKA
2 t POPPY SEEDS
I T CAPERS
SALT TO TASTE

Hungarian Noodles
Serves 2

Cook the pasta according to instructions on packet. Drain and mix in the sour cream. Gently reheat to piping hot, stir in paprika, poppy seeds and capers, and serve with a colorful salad.

Variation:

Substitute nutmeg for the paprika, but use slightly less.

"In the preparation of white flour one sacrifices most of the vital elements of the whole grain. Phosphates, calcium, magnesium, iron, silicum, iodine and manganese, vitamins, the precious vitamin E, and innumerable natural ferments and enzymes — not forgetting the very germ of the wheat — all are lost in the process of 'refining' the flour."

— Lima food catalog

Wheat Gluten

Gluten is the ingredient in wheat that makes it elastic. The Chinese make it into a thick, tasty paste that can be used in vegetarian dishes to give a texture and flavor reminiscent of poultry. They call it, in fact, Mock Duck. You can make your own gluten from gluten flour, available in health food stores, but it is more convenient to buy it ready-made in cans from Chinese stores. It can be used in stews, soups and pies, and in Oriental dishes such as egg rolls and spring rolls, pilau rice and curry. In Japan it is called seitan. Most of the recipes in this book use canned gluten, but there is a delicious start-from-scratch recipe on page 40.

Oats

Whole oats are rarely eaten, but the grain can be bought coarsely or finely ground, and it is the medium or fine oatmeal which is the best for making porridge. Porridge made with oatmeal takes a lot longer than if flakes are used, but for this reason, the oatmeal porridge is sweeter and creamier. For every cupful of water use a handful of oats and a pinch of salt; simmer for about 30 minutes and stir often.

Oat flakes make delicious cakes and flapjacks, and the flakes added to bread make it damp and sweet. Oats for muesli should be soaked a few hours before use; this makes them taste creamier and richer.

Oats are probably the most nutritious of all the grains except buckwheat, as they contain protein in a form which is easy for the body to use. They are also rich in silicon, a mineral essential for the development of muscles, brain, and nerve structure. Oats are also said to reduce blood pressure. In Scotland they are used to make Oatcakes (p.166).

> *"Eat slowly; only men in rags*
> *And gluttons old in sin*
> *Mistake themselves for carpet bags*
> *And tumble victuals in."*

> — Sir Walter Raleigh

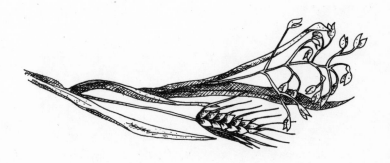

Chapter 3

Beans

There are many different varieties of beans and peas which are collectively known as pulses. They are a rich source of protein in a vegetarian diet. Unlike animal proteins (milk and cheese) the protein of pulse foods is not always in perfect balance if they are eaten alone. To obtain high quality protein, beans should be eaten at the same meal as a whole grain, e.g. brown rice, millet, wholewheat bread. The beans and grains complement each other to release as much as 30% more protein for the body to use than if they were eaten separately.

How to Cook Beans:

Beans should always be picked over to remove stones and then thoroughly rinsed. Bring them to a boil with 4 to 5 times their own volume in water, and simmer in a covered pot until soft, adding more water if necessary. Salt should be added near the end of cooking, or the beans will take longer to soften. If the beans are soaked overnight before cooking, they will partly soften, and the cooking times will be half to three-quarters of the times given in the recipes. The soaking water should not be used for cooking. Feed it to your house plants. Dry beans can also be cooked in a pressure cooker in $2\frac{1}{2}$ times their volume of water, and the cooking times will be approximately the same as for pre-soaked beans. All beans improve with longer cooking than the times given, which are a minimum. With longer cooking, they get creamier and tastier. In general, most beans are bland when eaten alone. However, once cooked they can be used as an ingredient in thousands of delicious vegetarian recipes, and if you have too many, they freeze well. Another useful general rule: 1 C dry beans makes about 2 C cooked.

Adzuki Beans

Small, oval, and dark red in color, these beans grow in the Far East. They are said to be good for the kidneys and are used there for their medicinal properties as much as for food. Cooking time: 1 hour.

Blackeyed Peas

These are smallish, buff-colored beans with a black spot. Cooking time: 45 minutes.

Blackeyed Peas in Herb Sauce
Serves 4-5

1 1/2 OZ (1/3 STICK) BUTTER
1 T DRIED PARSLEY OR 2T FRESH, FINELY CHOPPED
1 BAY LEAF
1/2 t SAGE
1/4 t THYME
1 t MARJORAM
2 C MILK
2 C COOKED BLACKEYED PEAS
2 T CORNSTARCH DISSOLVED IN 3 TO 4 T COLD WATER
SALT AND FRESH BLACK PEPPER

Melt the butter in a heavy saucepan and gently fry the herbs in it for one or two minutes to seal in the aromatic oils in the herbs. Add the milk and blackeyed peas and re-heat to almost boiling. Add cornstarch, stirring constantly until the sauce thickens. Season with salt and pepper and serve with a grain and vegetables.

Butter Beans

These are large, white kidney-shaped beans. They are good served in a creamy sauce. You can use them in the herb sauce recipe above, for example. Cooking time: 1 1/4 to 1 1/2 hours.

2 T FRESH CHOPPED PARSLEY

$^1/_2$ t MARJORAM

$^1/_2$ t SAGE

$^1/_4$ t THYME

$^1/_2$ t PAPRIKA

$^1/_2$ t GROUND CORIANDER SEED

I T BUTTER

2 C SOFT COOKED BUTTER BEANS

$^1/_3$ C SOUR CREAM

SALT AND PEPPER TO TASTE

Butter Bean Mash
Serves 2-3

Fry the herbs and spices gently in the butter for 1 to 2 minutes. Add the beans, mashing them into the herbs. Add sour cream and re-heat gently. Season to taste. This mash can be eaten with a grain or used as a pie crust or sandwich filling.

Chickpeas

Chickpeas are also called garbanzo beans. Gram peas are similar to chickpeas, only a little smaller. They are widely used in India in Bombay Mix, and also ground into a fine flour called besan, which is excellent for making batter. The batter recipe given below, for pancakes, can also be used for Pakora (p. 102) and for coating vegetables to make the deep-fried delicacy Tempura (p. 81). Cooking time: 1 $^1/_2$ to 2 hours, at least. Longer is better, and a pressure cooker is almost essential to avoid burning accidents.

I C SOFT COOKED CHICKPEAS

2 T TAHINI

I T OIL

JUICE OF I LEMON

$^1/_2$ t PAPRIKA

SALT AND PEPPER

Hummus
This is a delicious Middle Eastern dip/spread.
Serves 3-4

Blend all ingredients Hummus goes well with salad, or as a spread for bread or a dip for chips.

2 **C** GRAM (CHICKPEA OR GARBANZO)
    FLOUR
2 t BAKING POWDER
I **C** MILK
¹/₂ **C** WATER
I **T** SOY SAUCE
¹/₂ t GROUND CORIANDER SEED
I t SAGE
I t MILD **M**ADRAS CURRY POWDER
¹/₄ t WHOLE CUMIN SEED
¹/₈ t CHILI POWDER
¹/₄ t POWDERED GINGER
SALT TO TASTE
OIL (FOR FRYING)

Gram Flour Pancakes
Makes eight 6-inch pancakes

Blend all ingredients in a blender, and set aside for 10 to 15 minutes to allow to thicken and congeal to eliminate sticking. In a heavy skillet or frying pan over a gentle heat, warm 1 T oil and drop in a small ladleful of batter. The pan should be hot enough so that the underside is browned and the top side is congealed after about 50 seconds. Turn over and brown the top side (now underneath) for about 30 seconds. Keep warm in the oven. Repeat until you have enough. These pancakes are delicious with a spicy tofu filling and a tomato sauce. Children love them.

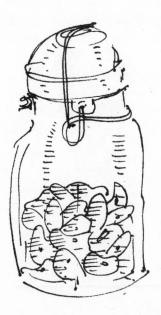

Haricot Beans

Haricots are the beans used in Boston baked beans, so you have probably eaten them before. Cooking time: 1 hour.

$^1/_2$ **t BASIL**

$^1/_2$ **t OREGANO**

$^1/_2$ **t THYME**

$^1/_2$ **t GROUND CORIANDER SEED**

I BAY LEAF

$^1/_3$ **STICK BUTTER**

2 C COOKED HARICOTS

2 C MILK

2 T CORNSTARCH, DISSOLVED IN MILK

I SMALL CAN TOMATO PASTE

$^1/_2$ **C GRATED CHEDDAR CHEESE**

SALT AND PEPPER TO TASTE

Note: Other beans that work well in this recipe are lima beans and white kidney beans.

Haricot Beans in Tomato Sauce
Serves 4-6

Fry the herbs gently in the butter in a saucepan for 1 to 2 minutes, then add the beans with the milk. Dissolve the cornstarch in a little cold milk and bring the beans back to a boil. When nearly boiling, add the cornstarch gradually, and stir until thick. Add the tomato paste and cook gently 1 minute longer, stirring constantly. Add the cheese and stir until dissolved. Add the soy sauce. Season the sauce with salt and pepper and serve. This is delicious over rice and stir-fried vegetables, especially dark greens.

Lima Beans

Limas look like butter beans, but are much smaller. Serve them with a sauce such as herb, cheese or tomato sauce. Cooking time: 1 ½ hours.

Marrowfat Peas

Marrowfats are whole dried peas, green in color. They are good in vegetable stews. They can also be bought split in half, in which case they cook more quickly but don't keep their shape. Cooking time for whole peas is 1 ½ hours or more.

Mung Beans

These tiny round olive-green beans are very tasty and good for soups and pies. The Chinese sprout these. In India they are made into Dal (p. 103), a bean stew. Cooking time: 45 minutes.

Lentils

Lentils were used by the Romans, whose armies carried them as a food supply because they were said to be good for fighting men. Cooking time: brown lentils 45 minutes, green lentils 1 hour, red lentils 25 to 35 minutes. Pick them over before cooking to remove small stones. Use 2 C lentils and at least 5 C water (more for longer cooking) to avoid burning accidents. Stir often when they begin to soften.

Red Kidney Beans

Dark red in color, these beans have a rich flavor which makes a vegetable stew or pie delicious. The juice from the cooking is also rich and thick and can be used in gravies. Red beans are used in the Mexican dish Chili Con Carne (p. 65) and to make Red Bean Goulash (p. 62). Cooking time: 1 hour.

Note: These beans contain a natural toxin and must always be boiled for at least ten minutes.

Split Peas

There are two types of split peas: yellow and green. They differ slightly in flavor; the green ones taste more like garden peas. These are very tasty and can be used for fritters, soups, stews, and pies. 1 C dry peas will make 2 ½ C soaked, but the cooked quantity will depend on how thick they are. Cooking time: 1 to 1 ½ hours.

Soybeans

Soybeans contain a protein of higher quality than in any other plant food, and when eaten with a whole grain, this protein is in perfect balance. Soybeans have a distinct rich flavor. They should always be pre-soaked before cooking, or the cooking time is at least 4 hours. After soaking, cook 2 ½ to 3 hours; in a pressure cooker 1 to 1 ½ hours. They can then be used in stews and pies or mixed together with grains.

TVP is textured vegetable protein derived from soybeans, made to look and taste like meat. TVP cooks up quickly, especially if soaked 15 to 20 minutes beforehand. Try using it in tomato sauces, stews, and vegetables; it's also a good standby for a visit from non-vegetarian family members. My children like it cooked into tomato sauce which is then used for Lasagna (p. 118).

Sprouting Beans and Peas

Nearly all beans, also some seeds and grains, will sprout, and their mineral and vitamin content, especially vitamin C, is greatly increased. When a seed sprouts, it is expressing the life and potential for growth within it. It is also providing us with unsprayed and untreated nutrients 100% fresh. The best and easiest sprouts are made with wheat grains, alfalfa seeds, mung beans (Chinese bean sprouts), chickpeas, green lentils, and fenugreek seeds. You can use them in salads, or add to sautéed vegetables just before serving, as the Chinese do. Wheat sprouts can be used to improve the flavor and nutrients in homemade bread. Add them to the dough before it is put to rise.

How to Make Sprouts:

Rinse about 1 C of the seeds, place in a bowl and cover with lukewarm water. Stand them overnight. In the morning, rinse the seeds and put them into large jars — only a few to each jar because they are really going to grow. Cover the tops with gauze or paper and put in a warm dark place. Leave for 3 to 5 days, rinsing them in fresh water 3 times daily. (You can also buy sprouting racks in some whole food stores.) When ready, they should be eaten quickly, but will keep in a fridge for a few days.

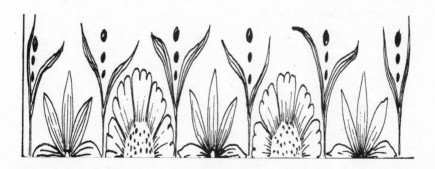

Tofu

Tofu is soybean curd. It is like a cheese made from the milk of the soybeans when they are ground and boiled in water. It has been used in the Far East for thousands of years as a staple food, just as pasta and bread have been used as a staple from wheat in the West. Tofu is a complete protein food superior to animal protein, since it is much easier to digest. It is also an ideal diet food, having the lowest ratio of calories to protein of any food except bean sprouts. It does not contain cholesterol. Tofu is also a good convenience food, ready to eat when you buy it. If you compare its nutritional contents with those of meat, you will be surprised at how nutritious it is. Tofu can be eaten as it is in salads or sandwiches. You can mash it up like cottage cheese and add spices (paprika and fenugreek are good ones). You can also sauté it in oil with a pinch of thyme, paprika, curry powder, sage, and some soy sauce, then serve it with rice and vegetables.

2 T OIL (FOR SAUTÉING)
1 1/2 C COOKED BROWN RICE OR
   MASHED POTATOES
1 t THYME
1 t SAGE
2 C MASHED TOFU
3 T TOMATO PASTE
SALT AND PEPPER
1 TO 2 t WHOLE GRAIN MUSTARD
4 LARGE GREEN PEPPERS, HALVED
   VERTICALLY AND SEEDED
1 C GRATED CHEDDAR CHEESE

Tofu Stuffed Green Peppers

Serves 4

Preheat oven to 250°. Sauté the rice and herbs in a skillet and add the tofu, mashing it up in the pan. Fry for about 2 minutes, then add the tomato paste, seasoning and mustard. Mix well. Coat the skins of the green peppers with oil and fill them with the mixture. Arrange them on a baking tray, sprinkle with cheese and bake 20 minutes at 250°.

Chapter 4

Vegetables

If you can, get organically grown vegetables, either from your own garden or a local farm or co-op. You will probably prefer them to those grown with chemical fertilizers and pesticides. They are much more flavorful and are not always more expensive. Most vegetables are rich in minerals and vitamins and there is growing evidence that a diet rich in fresh raw fruits and vegetables helps prevent cancer. However, vegetables are delicate organisms and their nutrients can be destroyed very easily. Try to get them as fresh as possible, cut them only immediately before eating or cooking, and cook them carefully.

How to Cook Vegetables:

Don't boil! It is better to steam them in a wire basket suspended in a covered pot containing 1 to 2 inches of boiling water, or you can buy a special vegetable steamer for the same purpose. Sautéing vegetables is the best way to prepare them for cooking in soups and stews. The vegetables contain aromatic oils which make them tasty, and during cooking these will tend to evaporate and be lost. By sautéing briefly in hot oil (just stir them round and round in the oil for a few minutes in a heavy saucepan) the aromatic oils dissolve into the cooking oil and cannot evaporate. This process will also seal in the vitamins and minerals that would otherwise evaporate and be lost. If you must boil vegetables, always save the nutrient-laden water for use in other recipes. Simmer slowly and keep the pot covered. All root vegetables can be wrapped in foil and baked whole in a tray containing a little water to prevent them drying up. This is a gentle cooking method which leaves the delicate nutrients sealed inside the vegetable.

Asparagus

Asparagus spears are the stems and leaves of the plant. Cut off the stalks just below the tip, where the tiny green leaves grow. Cut the stalks 1 ½ inches long and steam them for 5 to 10 minutes until nearly tender. Then add the delicate leafy sections and steam a further 4 to 5 minutes or until tender. Serve immediately — traditionally, with melted butter.

Globe Artichokes

The artichoke is a member of the thistle family. Artichokes were a delicacy for the ancient Romans, who preserved them in honey and vinegar. Steam the artichokes whole, adding a little olive oil and vinegar to the water. They're cooked when the leaves come away from the base easily. Serve them whole, with a bowl of melted butter. Peel off a leaf at a time and dip it in the butter; the part at the base of the leaf is the part to eat. When you get to the middle, watch out for the choke. Don't eat it. Underneath it is the heart, which is good to eat.

Jerusalem Artichokes

These are knobby little root vegetables, very difficult to clean. They have a strong and distinctive flavor. For this reason, it is best to cook them alone, otherwise all the other vegetables will taste of artichoke. They can be steamed, baked or fried. You can bake artichokes whole in the oven, like potatoes, but with very uneven artichokes this can be tricky, as the knobby parts cook more quickly than the middle. They take longer than potatoes to soften.

2 ¹/₂ C Jerusalem artichokes
1 ¹/₂ oz butter for sauteing
Approximately 4 C nutmeg sauce
   (P. 96)

Artichokes in Nutmeg Sauce
Serves 6

Slice the artichokes about ¹/₂-inch thick and sauté them very gently in the butter until tender: about 30 minutes. Stir frequently to avoid sticking, adding a little water if necessary. Make a nutmeg sauce. (Garam masala is also good in the sauce instead of nutmeg.) When the artichokes are tender, pour the sauce over them, and cook for 5 minutes, continuing to stir them. These are delicious over brown rice. Try this recipe also with sweet potato or parsnips instead of the artichokes.

Artichoke Allumettes

Cut artichokes up into little match sticks. Fry quickly. Children love them. Also try chopping them bigger and deep-frying them like french fries.

Fresh Green Beans and Peas

Make sure the beans you buy are young, crisp, and not stringy. Remove the top, tail, and string, and in some cases the pod, after which most varieties are delicious gently steamed and tossed in butter and salt. Mangetouts (snow peas) should not be steamed. They are crisp, sweet, and a delicate pale green in color. The pods are absolutely flat, and as the French name suggests, you eat the whole thing. They are lovely in salads when fresh, or served with dips at a buffet. Another legume delicious raw is the sugar snap pea. These are also delicious if stir-fried very briefly in a wok, Chinese style. Try them this way with sliced water chestnuts, a small pinch of freshly grated ginger root, and a squeeze of lemon.

Beets

Beets and their juice are said to be very good for cleansing the blood. Raw beets can be boiled whole in their skins and peeled afterwards (this seals in the flavor and goodness and makes the peeling easier) or simply baked in a moderate oven, wrapped up. Small ones take an hour or two, big ones up to 3 to 4 hours.

2 LARGE OR 4 MEDIUM COOKED BEETS
PINCH OF SALT
2 T CIDER VINEGAR
1 T BUTTER
FRESHLY MILLED BLACK PEPPER TO TASTE

Sour Beets
Serves 2-4

Peel and chop the beets finely. Place in a pan with a pinch of salt and vinegar and simmer covered until most of the liquid is evaporated. Add the butter and black pepper. Serve with Cottage Pie (p. 80).

2 LARGE OR 3 TO 4 MEDIUM COOKED BEETS
1 T BUTTER (FOR SAUTÉING)
SALT AND FRESHLY MILLED BLACK PEPPER TO TASTE
2 T FRESH PARSLEY, CHOPPED FINE

Beets with Parsley Butter
Serves 2-4

Peel and chop the beets. Melt the butter in a saucepan and briefly sauté the beets. Add salt and serve with a sprinkle of black pepper and the parsley.

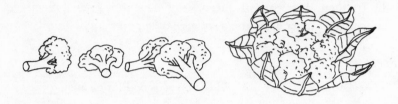

Broccoli

Steam the florets gently taking care not to overcook. Delicious with a delicate sauce. Broccoli can be used instead of cauliflower to make Broccoli au Gratin (see Cauliflower au Gratin, p. 42) and in soups, stews, pies, and casseroles. Always add broccoli later than other vegetables to reduce the risk of overcooking.

Brussel Sprouts

Good sprouts should be small and firm when pressed. When preparing them, don't cut crosswise on the base, as this allows the juice to run out. Simply remove a few outer leaves and steam them until just tender. Sprout tops are good, too. They are the broad, spoon-shaped leaves that grow at the top of the plant. Use them in any recipe calling for leafy green vegetables.

"Good King Wenceslas looked out
On his vegetable garden.
He bumped into a Brussels sprout
And said, 'I beg your pardon.'"

— Anadinath

Cabbage

Spring cabbage and the curly savoys can be chopped up and steamed. Drumheads are the hard, pale green type which are good for salads, and Chinese cabbages are long and pointed in shape. Both these types are, if to be cooked, best shredded and sautéed until translucent. If you like caraway seeds, you could add a few just before the end of cooking. Nutmeg Sauce (p. 96) goes very well with sautéed cabbage. There is a type of cabbage which is bright purple in color. If you slice it in half, you will see beautiful patterns in the leaves. Whole cabbage leaves can be steamed and then stuffed. Place a spoonful of the stuffing (spiced leftover grains, for instance) by the base of each leaf and roll it up in a bundle. Brush with oil and bake a little until hot again.

PINCH OF FRESHLY GROUND CLOVES AND NUTMEG

¹/₄ t THYME

¹/₂ t CINNAMON

I T OIL (FOR SAUTÉING)

I LARGE RED CABBAGE (ABOUT 2 lbs.), CHOPPED SMALL

3 SOUR BAKING APPLES, CHOPPED SMALL

JUICE AND A LITTLE RIND FROM A LEMON

Red Cabbage and Apple
Serves 4-6

Sauté the spices in a saucepan for a minute in the oil, then add the red cabbage, the apples, and the lemon juice and rind with a small amount of water. Simmer gently for 30 minutes, stirring often. Just before serving, it's nice to stir in a little thick cream.

I SMALL WHITE CABBAGE, SHREDDED
I T OIL (FOR SAUTÉING)
4 T SHREDDED FRESH COCONUT
¹/₂ T TAMARIND PASTE DISSOLVED
   IN **2 t** WATER
SALT TO TASTE

Indian Cabbage
Serves 2-3

Sauté the cabbage in oil for 1 minute, and add coconut and tamarind. Cover and cook slowly until cabbage is tender. Add salt to taste. Serve with rice.

Carrots

Brightly colored, inexpensive, tasty, nutritious, and versatile, carrots can be eaten raw, steamed, roasted, baked, mashed, and sautéed. Carrots have many qualities and can find their way into almost any type of food. As most of the flavor of carrots is in the skin or just under it, if they are organically grown they should never be scraped or peeled. However, most supermarket carrots have pesticides in the skin, and so should be peeled (often the skin is bitter because of this). To bake, wrap whole carrots in foil or oiled paper and bake at 250° for about 1 ¹/₂ hours. To steam, place whole carrots in a steamer basket until about half cooked. Transfer to a shallow baking tray. Coat with oil and sprinkle with thyme and a pinch of sea or rock salt. Bake at 250° until soft and beginning to crisp. Chopped cooked carrots are a nice addition to savory fried rice. Carrots can also be used in puddings and cakes.

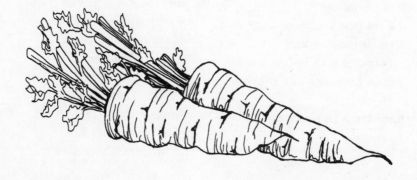

2 **C** BABY CARROTS
WATER
I **T** BUTTER
SALT AND FRESHLY GROUND BLACK
  PEPPER TO TASTE
PINCH OF FINELY CHOPPED FRESH
  MINT

Glazed Carrots
Serves 4-6

In a heavy saucepan, boil the carrots in very little water, adding the butter, salt and pepper at the beginning. Make sure the carrots never boil dry. When they are tender, allow them to simmer very gently in the butter for about 10 minutes. (If you have a double boiler you can use it to do this.) Remove the carrots from the pan and serve them sprinkled with finely chopped mint.

6 TO 8 MEDIUM CARROTS
I **T** BUTTER (FOR SAUTÉING)
3 TO 4 **C** WATER
I **T** HONEY
2 **T** APPLE CIDER VINEGAR
2 **T** CORNSTARCH
SALT TO TASTE

Sweet and Sour Carrots
Serves 6

Grate the carrots or slice them very thinly. Briefly sauté in butter in a heavy saucepan, cover with water and simmer until tender. When almost cooked, add the honey and vinegar. Blend the cornstarch in a little cold water and add it to the pan. Stir until thick. Continue to simmer all the ingredients together for a few minutes so that the flavors can blend. You can adjust the sweet and sour flavor to your own taste, as this recipe is quite mildly flavored. A good way to eat sweet and sour carrots is with French fries and some crumbled cheese. Fussy children might just be persuaded to eat carrots this way. They go well with dark greens too.

SEITAN:

¹/₂ **C** TAMARI (SOY SAUCE)
³/₄ TO **1 C** WATER
2 ¹/₂ **C** GLUTEN FLOUR
1 ¹/₃ **C** WHOLE WHEAT FLOUR
1 ¹/₂ t THYME
¹/₂ t GALANGAL (P. 198)
1 t SAGE
DASH OF SALT
7 TO 8 t oil

Sweet and Sour Carrots with Seitan
Serves 8

Mix tamari with water. Place dry ingredients in a large bowl and add the liquid. Knead to an elastic dough and until all the ingredients are thoroughly blended. On a floured board roll out the dough to about ³/₄-inch thick. With a sharp knife, cut it into ¹/₂-inch wide strips. Then cut the strips into short pieces about one or two inches long. These are now small pieces of seitan.

In a heavy skillet, heat about half the oil until a piece of seitan sizzles. Fry the seitan on both sides until golden, removing the pieces with a spatula as they cook and filling the pan with raw seitan and more oil. Set the fried seitan aside.

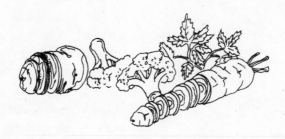

6-7 MEDIUM CARROTS
3 T OIL
2 T COARSELY GRATED FRESH GINGER
  ROOT
I t GROUND ANISE SEED
7 ½ C WATER
⅓ C CIDER VINEGAR
3 T SOFT BROWN SUGAR
2 T TAMARI (SOY SAUCE)

Now make the following:
Cut the carrots into long, narrow pieces. In a large stockpot, sauté them briefly in the oil with ginger and aniseed. Add the water, vinegar, sugar and tamari and bring to a boil. When it boils, add the fried seitan, cover and simmer 45 minutes until the water is reduced to a gravy and the flavors are nicely blended. Season lightly with salt and serve hot with a green vegetable.

Sesame Carrots

Slice some raw carrots very thin and sauté very gently in oil with sesame seeds and a little honey.

Carrots in Sauce

Make an Herb Sauce to go with your carrots (p. 95).

Cauliflower

Cauliflower can be steamed whole, including some of the tiny green leaves. The cauliflower is done when a sharp knife slides into the base with just a slight pressure. Cooked cauliflower soon loses its delicate flavor and should be eaten immediately.

I MEDIUM CAULIFLOWER
¹/₃ STICK OF BUTTER
3 T WHOLE WHEAT FLOUR
3 C MILK
¹/₄ t NUTMEG
SALT AND PEPPER TO TASTE
I C GRUYERE CHEESE (CHEDDAR IS OKAY)
I C PARMESAN CHEESE
I C BREAD CRUMBS
¹/₂ OZ BUTTER

Cauliflower au Gratin
Serves 4

Steam the cauliflower until not quite tender. In a heavy saucepan, make a roux by melting the butter, whisking in the flour, and very slowly adding milk, stirring as it thickens. Add the nutmeg, salt, and pepper. Bring to a very gentle boil, stirring, and simmer for 2 minutes. Remove from heat. Grate the cheese and add 2 T of each kind to the crumbs. Add the rest of the cheese to the sauce and beat well until very creamy. Add the cauliflower to the sauce. Re-heat, season with salt and pour into an oiled, preheated casserole dish. Sprinkle with bread crumbs and dots of butter and broil until the crumb crust is crisp. My mother used to cook the cauliflower for an au gratin by simmering it gently in the milk she would be using to make the sauce. This is a wonderful idea, but it does take a little longer.

Celery

Possibly the nicest way to eat celery is to soak it in chilled water for 15-20 minutes and then serve it raw with a dip. Cooked celery is an important ingredient in winter soups, stews, and pies. There is a variety of celery which is grown exclusively for the root, which is called celeriac. It is the size of a large beet with a very rough gray skin and white flesh. It is hard to find, but if you are lucky enough to have a vegetable garden, you may be familiar with it. Celeriac is delicious raw in salads and cooked in soups and stews.

4 CELERY HEARTS

4 BIG PANCAKES (P. 157)

2 C CHEESE SAUCE (P. 95)

2 t PAPRIKA

I C GRATED PARMESAN CHEESE
(CHEDDAR IS OKAY)

Celery Pancakes
Serves 4

Make the pancake batter. Steam the whole celery hearts for about 10 minutes. Make the cheese sauce. Fry up a plate of pancakes and set aside. When the celery is tender, wrap each celery heart in a pancake. Lay the rolls side by side in a casserole dish. Season the cheese sauce with paprika and pour it over the celery. Sprinkle the top with parmesan cheese and brown the casserole in the oven at 350° for about 10 minutes.

Chard

A juicy, leafy summer vegetable resembling spinach, but with a more delicate flavor, chard is lovely in salad. My favorite way to cook it is to sauté the shredded leaves in oil with a pinch of whole cumin seed, curry powder, paprika, rubbed sage, and a little salt. Very little oil is necessary; the plant cooks in its own juice.

Eggplant

These are usually sautéed, and they absorb a lot of the oil. If they are cut into rounds 30 minutes before use and are sprinkled with salt, a dark, bitter liquid will emerge which can be poured off and thrown away. The flavor will be better and the eggplant will not be so oily when cooked. Sauté them until translucent and soft. Alternatively, bake them whole, well-wrapped, in the oven.

	Tofu and Eggplant
4 TO 5 C (I LARGE) EGGPLANT, PREPARED WITH SALT AS ABOVE	Serves 4-6
4 T OIL (FOR SAUTÉING)	
I PACK (I lb) TOFU	Heat oil in a large skillet and
½ t GROUND GINGER	sauté eggplant for 5 to 6
½ t ASAFETIDA (HING) (P.196)	minutes. Cut tofu into 1-inch
PINCH CHILI POWDER	cubes and add with spices,
I lb CAN TOMATOES	tomatoes, and soy sauce. Cook
2 T SOY SAUCE	gently until eggplant is
SALT TO TASTE	translucent. Season and cook a
FRESHLY MILLED BLACK PEPPER	few more minutes.

Fennel

Fennel has a delicious flavor, reminiscent of anise. The seeds are used as a spice. The bulb is pale green and layered like an onion, and makes delicious salad. Alternatively, it can be steamed and served with butter or a delicate sauce.

Kale

This is a curly, dark green leafy vegetable with a strong, delicious flavor. Get fresh, crisp kale, chop the leaves, and steam them. Kale goes well as a vegetable with pies and sauces. The young leaves are good in salad.

Kohlrabi

These are not root vegetables, but the swollen stalk of a leafy plant. The skin is usually pale green or dark red, the inside white. They taste very like turnips. Use them in stews or in combinations of sautéed vegetables.

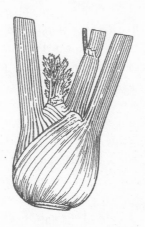

Parsnips

Wrap parsnips whole in foil and bake at 200° about 1 to 1½ hours until soft. Alternatively, roast them as you would potatoes, sprinkling them with sea salt and a pinch of thyme beforehand. They will cook faster than potatoes if roasted in the oven. For quick roast parsnips, steam parsnips beforehand until partly cooked, then brush with oil, sprinkle with sea salt and thyme, and finish by roasting. They are also nice when steamed until soft and then placed on a baking tray, sprinkled with grated cheese, and browned in the oven. Try making sesame parsnips — same method as for Sesame Carrots (p. 41).

To Dress Parsnips:
Here's some advice from long ago:

> *"Scrape well three or four large roots, cleansing well their outside, and cutting off as much of the little end as is Fibrous, and of the great end as is Hard. Put them into a possnet or pot, with about a quart of milk upon them, or as much as will cover them in boiling, which do moderately till you find they are tender. This may be in an hour and a half, sooner or later, as the roots are of good kind. Then take them out, and scrape all the outside into a pulp, like the pulp of roasted apples which put in a dish upon a chafing dish of coals, with a little of the milk you boiled them in, put to them; not so much as to drown them, but only to imbibe them and then with stewing, the pulp will imbibe all that Milk. When you see it is drunk in, put to the pulp a little more of the same Milk and stew that, till it be drunk in. Continue doing this till it hath drunk in a good quantity of the Milk, and is well swelled with it, and will take no more, which may be in a good half hour. Eat them so, without Sugar or Butter, for they will have a natural sweetness, that is beyond Sugar, and will be Unctuous, so as not to need Butter."*

— Sir Kenelm Digby, 1669

Fresh Green Peas

Pod the peas and steam them with a little mint and salt, and maybe a little honey. For 4 people you need about 2 to 3 pounds of pods, depending on their fatness, which indicates how many peas are inside.

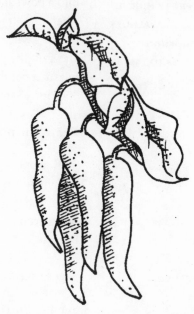

Peppers

Sweet green and red bell peppers have a multitude of culinary uses. They brighten up vegetable stews, pies, sauces, and salads and are very rich in vitamin C. To prepare, cut off the stalk and calyx, and cut out the seeds and white fibers in the center. Throw this part away. The pepper can then be cut into decorative rings, chopped fine or stuffed.

Stuffed Peppers

Halve 4 green peppers vertically and remove seeds to make 8 hollow shells. Steam the peppers until not quite soft. They are then ready for stuffing. There are several ways to stuff green peppers; the following are only a few suggestions.

2 C COOKED BUCKWHEAT (P. 14)
2 STICKS CELERY
2 T OIL
¹/₂ t GROUND CUMIN
¹/₂ t GROUND CORIANDER
2 T FRESH PARSLEY, FINELY MINCED
¹/₄ C ROAST PEANUTS OR WALNUTS
2 MEDIUM TOMATOES, SKINNED
SALT AND BLACK PEPPER TO TASTE

Buckwheat Stuffing

Chop the celery fine and sauté it in the oil with the herbs, spices, and nuts. Chop the tomatoes into a bowl and add the celery when it is almost soft. Mix in the buckwheat, salt and pepper, and stuff the peppers with this mixture. Oil the skins. Bake at 350° for 15 minutes.

Bean Stuffing

Stuff peppers with haricot beans in Tomato Sauce (p. 97). This one can be mixed with some bread crumbs to thicken it up. Bake at 350° for 15 minutes.

3 C SWEET CORN KERNELS
¹/₂ C MILK
I OZ (**¹/₄** STICK) BUTTER
I C GRATED CHEDDAR OR GRUYERE
   CHEESE
SALT, PEPPER, AND CAYENNE PEPPER
   TO TASTE

Sweet Corn Stuffing

Simmer the corn gently in the milk and butter until tender. Add salt and pepper. If you use fresh corn, scrape it off the cob. When it softens, add the cheese and a pinch of cayenne pepper. Cook gently until the cheese dissolves and stuff the peppers with this mixture. Bake at 350° for 15 minutes.

Potato Stuffing

Stuff peppers with mashed potato, chopped tomatoes, and oregano. Bake at 350° for 15 minutes.

2 T OIL (FOR SAUTÉING)
1 ¹/₂ C COOKED BROWN RICE OR
   MASHED POTATOES
1 t THYME
1 t SAGE
2 C MASHED TOFU
3 T TOMATO PASTE
SALT AND PEPPER
1 TO 2 WHOLE GRAIN MUSTARD

Tofu Stuffing

Sauté the rice and herbs in a skillet and add the tofu, mashing it up in the pan. Fry for about 2 minutes, then add the tomato paste, seasoning and mustard. Mix well. Bake at 350° for 15 minutes.

Potatoes

There are many ways to cook potatoes, and many ways to use them when they're cooked. If you need to peel them it is better to wait until after they are cooked, as the skin seals in the flavor. Red potatoes are for boiling, steaming, and mashing. White potatoes ("bakers") are best baked or roasted.

New Potatoes

Boil or steam them with salt and mint leaves. Serve whole with butter. It isn't necessary to peel them.

Baked Potatoes

Bake whole at 400° for an hour. Before baking, the skins can be rubbed with oil, which softens them, although some people prefer the skins to be crisp. Young potatoes, or those with very scarred skins, should not be baked.

Roasted Potatoes

Place potatoes whole or halved in a baking tray with a good coating of oil and sprinkled with sea salt and thyme or rosemary. Bake at 375° until soft inside, making sure they are always coated with oil. For really crisp skins, try the following: boil the potatoes until partly cooked, then cool. Peel, and score the surface with the prongs of a fork. Put in a baking pan with oil and finish by roasting in the usual way. The extra trouble is worthwhile if you like really crisp roasted potatoes.

Mashed Potatoes

Boil or steam the potatoes until soft. You may choose to peel them or not. Mash them, adding a little butter and milk. Other nice additions are:

- fresh chopped parsley
- oregano
- grated cheese (any variety)
- cream, fresh or sour, or yogurt
- black pepper
- mint leaves
- whole grain mustard

2 **C** MASHED POTATOES

¹/₂ **C** GRATED CHEDDAR CHEESE

1 t MARJORAM

¹/₂ t FINELY GRATED LEMON PEEL

¹/₂ t SAGE

1 oz (¹/₄ STICK) BUTTER

SALT AND PEPPER

OIL FOR FRYING

Potato Fritters
Makes about eight 2-inch fritters

Mix all ingredients (except the oil) thoroughly. Form into balls, flatten them into patties, and fry them in hot oil for a few minutes on each side. You can also make fritters like this using a mixture of carrots, parsnips, and potatoes, mashed together.

Stuffed Baked Potatoes

Bake some large white potatoes whole in the oven. When done, cut a slice from the side of each potato and carefully scoop out the soft inside with a spoon. Keep the hollow skins warm to avoid them going soggy. Mash the insides in a bowl with some salt, pepper, and a little sour cream or butter. Add something interesting. Here are some good stuffing mixtures. You can use up leftovers in this way too:

- Freshly cooked spinach and tomato with oregano
- Plenty of grated cheese — a strongly flavored one such as gruyere or parmesan — and some paprika and oregano
- Any leftover cooked beans such as haricots, chickpeas, and kidney beans, a little soy sauce and some thyme, sage, and marjoram
- Plenty of yogurt and chopped watercress
- Grated carrot mixed with sour cream and black pepper, and a little fresh mint
- Butter Bean Mash (p. 24)

It is fun to invent new stuffing mixtures according to taste, season, and convenience. Pile the stuffing back into the spuds to overflowing, and return to the oven for 10 minutes.

Rutabagas

Rutabagas are winter root vegetables, bright orange when cooked, and they have a strong earthy taste which is delicious in vegetable soups and stews. Here are two very nice things to do with a rutabaga.

Cheesy Rutabagas

Peel two or three small rutabagas and slice them into discs. Steam until almost cooked. Put the rutabaga rings in an oiled baking tray and sprinkle a fairly thick layer of cheddar cheese on each one. Let the cheese brown and melt over the rutabagas in a hot oven for 5 to 10 minutes. These are good with beets and Parsley Sauce (p. 96) and a grain.

Rutabaga Mash

Allow one small rutabaga or half a large one for each person. Peel and dice the rutabagas and steam until very tender. Now mash them up in a bowl like potatoes, adding salt and pepper, a little milk and butter, and a pinch of thyme. Mix them until smooth and soft, and serve as a side vegetable to go with fritters or a pie. Try this recipe also with a half-and-half mix of carrot and rutabaga.

Seaweed

It's nicer than you think. Read the packet, and you'll be amazed at how much trouble it takes to process seaweed for culinary uses. Those early Japanese pioneers must have had amazing inspiration and optimism to develop such a delicious product from such an unlikely source. I have used arame in salads (see recipe, p. 129) and nori (sheet seaweed) to make Sushi (p. 110). A handful of prepared seaweed goes well with mixed, stir-fried, and simmered root vegetables such as carrots and parsnips. Follow the instructions on the packet, and then experiment a little with the cooked product.

Spinach

There are many nice ways to cook spinach. It should first be washed well and have some of the stalk cut off. Then chop the rest of the stalk finely, cut the leaves, and either steam or sauté it. Eat it simply, or make Spinach Pie (p. 67) or some Spinach Pancakes.

PANCAKE BATTER (SEE PANCAKES, P. 188)

2 lb SPINACH, WASHED CAREFULLY

1 T OIL (FOR SAUTÉING)

2 C GRATED CHEDDAR CHEESE

Spinach Pancakes
Serves 6 to 8

Mix up the pancake batter and set it in a cool place. Sauté the spinach, which will cook down in no time to much less than before, yielding maybe a half cup of juice. Save the juice to use as stock. Now make a pancake. Flip it on to a large flat plate and spread a layer of spinach over it. Cover with a layer of grated cheese. Continue making layers until you have a heap 6-inches high, then start another. Keep them warm and serve as soon as possible, cut into segments like a cake. Delicious with a spicy tomato sauce.

3 TO 4 MEDIUM RED POTATOES

1 ¹/₂ lb SPINACH

2 T OIL (FOR SAUTÉING)

4 TO 6 LARGE TOMATOES, QUARTERED

PINCH OF BASIL AND OREGANO

SALT AND FRESHLY GROUND BLACK PEPPER TO TASTE

Potatoes, Tomatoes, and Spinach
Serves 4-5

Boil the potatoes in their skins until well-cooked. When they're done, chop and sauté the spinach. When the spinach is nearly done, add the tomatoes and the herbs. Lots of vegetable juice comes out in the cooking. When the tomatoes soften, add the potatoes, thickly sliced, and cook all together slowly for 7 or 8 minutes. Serve with whole grain pasta and grated parmesan cheese.

Sweet Potatoes

These are starchy roots with a pinkish skin and delicate orange-yellow inside. They can be cut small and steamed to use in salads, or curried, or included with other vegetables in a bean stew. Like potatoes, they can be jacket-baked in the oven.

Squash

Until I came to America the only squash I ever saw were pumpkins and zucchini. I knew nothing of the lovely butternut and acorn squash that are so commonly grown in New York State. After several attempts to cook these unfamiliar vegetables, I came up with the following recipe, which is now one of my favorites.

3 C DICED BUTTERNUT SQUASH, SKIN
   AND SEEDS REMOVED
1 t GROUND CORIANDER SEED
1 ¹/₂ t SWEET GARAM MASALA (P. 199)
¹/₂ t GROUND ALLSPICE
¹/₄ t MACE
¹/₂ STICK OF BUTTER (FOR SAUTÉING)
4 C WATER
10 TO 15 LEAVES FRESH SWEET BASIL
SALT TO TASTE

Squashed Squash Soup
Serves 4

Sauté squash and spices in butter in a heavy saucepan. Add water and basil leaves, cover, and simmer until squash is soft, about 20 minutes. Crush pieces of squash against the sides of the pan with a wooden spoon so that the soup becomes a little thicker and richer. Season with salt and simmer, stirring constantly, a few minutes longer. Serve with cornbread.

Tomatoes

To peel tomatoes, place them into a large bowl and cover with boiling water for 15 to 20 seconds. Drain. The skins will peel off easily.

I BELL PEPPER, CHOPPED FINE

I STICK CELERY, CHOPPED FINE

2 OZ ('/₂ STICK) BUTTER OR '/₃ C
OIL (FOR SAUTÉING)

2 C SWEET CORN KERNELS

4 TOMATOES, QUARTERED

SALT AND PEPPER TO TASTE

4 LARGE TOMATOES, TOPS AND INSIDES
REMOVED

FILLING:

I C BREAD CRUMBS

I C GRATED GRUYERE OR OTHER
STRONG CHEESE

I OZ ('/₄ STICK) MELTED BUTTER

TOMATO INSIDES AND TOPS (FROM
ABOVE)

'/₂ C GRATED PARMESAN CHEESE

FRESHLY GROUND BLACK PEPPER TO
TASTE

Tomatoes on Toast

Serves 4

Soften the peppers and celery by sautéing in oil and then add the corn and tomatoes with the seasoning. Cook all together very gently for as long as you can spare — up to 1 hour if possible. If you have a double boiler it won't need to be watched. When you're getting really hungry, make some hot buttered toast. Pour the sauce over it and serve.

Stuffed Tomatoes

Try the recipes for buckwheat, sweet corn, mashed potato, and tofu stuffings (see pp. 48-49). Here is one more recipe.

Cheese Stuffed Tomatoes

Serves 4

Slice the tops off the tomatoes with a very sharp knife, and scoop out the interior. Combine all ingredients for the stuffing except the parmesan cheese, fill the tomatoes, and sprinkle the parmesan on top. Bake 10 to 15 minutes at 350° until the parmesan cheese sizzles.

Turnips

Turnips look like rutabagas but are smaller and more tender and the flesh is white in color. Their greens are tasty, and can be used in salads or gently steamed. The roots can be used in the same way as rutabagas, but the flavor is milder. Rosemary is a good herb to use with turnips. Try sautéing cooked turnip slices lightly in butter with a pinch of rosemary and sprinkling with fresh chopped parsley. Root vegetables such as carrots, parsnips, turnips, rutabagas, and potatoes can be cooked together in different combinations and then mashed up together with a little salt, pepper, butter, and cheese. The flavors of all these vegetables are subtly different and blend well together. This mixture, if left over, is also a good stuffing for tomatoes, sweet peppers, and the like.

Zucchini and Marrow

A vegetable marrow is very much like a large zucchini. Buy marrows in late summer and early fall, but avoid them after the end of September when they will be old with a tough shell and stringy, starchy flesh. If the zucchini is young, the skin can generally be eaten, but older ones need to be peeled. Remove the pips from the inside and chop the marrow into bite-sized pieces. These can now be steamed, or gently simmered in a little butter with some freshly chopped herbs —parsley, marjoram, or savory. Put a lid on the pan and allow the marrow to stew in its own juice.

Zucchini may also be baked "canoe style" with a stuffing: cut lengthwise, remove interior, and sauté with a grain or tofu and herbs. Fill the canoes, cover with foil, and bake gently in a slow oven. Try filling also with TVP, beans, cheese and bread crumbs, or nut mixtures. Young zucchinis are used in Ratatouille (p. 116). They may be sliced and gently cooked in butter or oil, or cut in half lengthwise and baked in a little butter or oil in a slow oven. Cooked this way, they look like little fish. They are a nice addition to tomato sauce, if sautéed gently for about 10 minutes in oil at the beginning of cooking before the tomatoes are added.

4 LARGE ZUCCHINI, HALVED LENGTHWISE

2 T OIL (FOR SAUTÉING)

5 OR 6 MEDIUM-SIZED TOMATOES, SKINNED AND QUARTERED

2 T CHOPPED ROASTED WALNUTS

2 C COOKED MILLET (P. 11) OR BUCKWHEAT (P. 14)

1/2 T SAGE

1/2 T CELERY SEED

PINCH OF CAYENNE PEPPER

1 T WHOLE GRAIN MUSTARD

SALT TO TASTE

Stuffed Zucchini Canoes
Serves 4

Scoop out the zucchini to make little canoes. Place the insides of the zucchini, chopped small, into a heavy skillet and sauté them in the oil with the tomatoes, nuts, mustard, herbs, and spices until translucent. Sir in the millet or buckwheat and mix well to make a stuffing for the canoes. Place the stuffing in the zucchini canoes and bake on an oiled tray at 350° until soft.

Chapter 5

Main Dishes

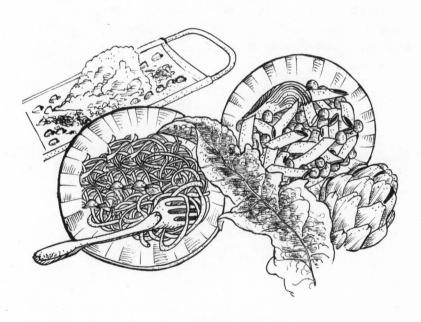

3 SMALL CARROTS

2 STICKS CELLERY

4 TO 5 LARGE TOMATOES

2 t PAPRIKA

I T GROUND CORIANDER SEED

I t OREGANO

3 T OIL (FOR SAUTÉING)

2 C COOKED RED KIDNEY BEANS

I TO 2 C WATER OR BEAN STOCK

I SMALL CAN WATER CHESTNUTS,
   WITH BRINE

JUICE OF I LEMON

I T HONEY

I TO 2 T CORNSTARCH, DISSOLVED IN
   WATER

SALT AND FRESHLY MILLED BLACK
   PEPPER TO TASTE

Red Bean Goulash
Serves 4-5

Chop the carrots, celery, and tomatoes and sauté them with the herbs and spices until nearly soft. Add a little water if necessary. Add the beans and water chestnuts, with their liquids, and the lemon juice and honey. Continue cooking until the vegetables are tender and the flavors are well-blended. Add cornstarch, stirring constantly, until the goulash thickens. Season with salt and pepper, and serve. This goes well with grated cheese or a grain, and a green salad.

2 **C** cooked chickpeas, plus 3 ¹/₂
C of the cooking water

1 **S**mall green or red bell pepper,
seeded and chopped

2 medium carrots, peeled and
sliced

¹/₂ small rutabaga or turnip,
peeled and chopped

2 or 3 red potatoes, chopped

2 sticks celery, chopped

2 bay leaves

¹/₂ t sage

¹/₂ t thyme

¹/₂ t rosemary

3 **T** oil (for sautéing)

¹/₄ to ¹/₂ small cauliflower, cut
in florets

3 **T** tahini

1 **T** cornstarch

1 t dried parsley or 2 **T** fresh

¹/₂ **C** chopped cilantro

Salt and pepper to taste

Chickpea Stew
Serves 4

Sauté all vegetables except the cauliflower with the dried herbs for 3 to 4 minutes. Add them to the chickpeas and stock in a large pan. Cover and simmer the stew for about 20 minutes, or until the vegetables are well-cooked. Add the cauliflower florets 10 minutes before the end of cooking. Add the tahini. Mix the cornstarch to a smooth paste in a little cold water and add it to the stew. Continue simmering a further 2 minutes, add fresh herbs, and season with salt and pepper. Serve with a grain or bread and butter.

I **C** DRY YELLOW SPLIT PEAS,
   SOAKED OVERNIGHT
2 BAY LEAVES
I t SAGE
I PINCH FRESHLY GROUND MACE
1²/₃ **C** HALVED BRUSSELS SPROUTS
¹/₂ SMALL RUTABAGA, PEELED AND
   DICED
2 CARROTS, PEELED AND DICED
I PARSNIP, PEELED AND DICED
SALT AND PEPPER TO TASTE

Split Pea Stew
Serves 4

Rinse the peas and put them on
to boil with the herbs, in twice
their volume of water. Simmer
for 30 minutes or until soft,
stirring regularly. Add more
water if necessary, but keep the
peas thick. Meanwhile, clean
and prepare the vegetables.
Dice the carrots, parsnips, and
rutabaga and cut outer leaves
from sprouts. Add all the
vegetables to the peas, cover,
and simmer very gently until
the vegetables are cooked,
adding more water as
necessary. Season with salt and
pepper and a pinch of mace.
Serve with sprigs of fresh
parsley and a pat of butter.

2 **C** RAW KIDNEY BEANS, SOAKED
  OVERNIGHT
I **C** SOY BEEF OR HAM PIECES **(TVP)**
I¹/₂ **C** DICED POTATO
I GREEN OR RED PEPPER, CHOPPED
I TO 2 STICKS CELERY, CHOPPED
2 CARROTS, PEELED AND SLICED
I **T** FRESHLY GROUND GINGER ROOT
³/₄ **T** GROUND CORIANDER SEEDS
2 WHOLE MILD RED CHILIS, FINELY
  CHOPPED
I **t** ASAFETIDA (HING) (P. 196)
3 **T** OIL (FOR SAUTÉING)
2 **T** YEAST EXTRACT OR
  4 **T** SOY SAUCE
I¹/₂ SMALL CANS TOMATO PASTE

Chili Con Carne
Serves 5-6

Rinse and cook the beans until soft. Meanwhile, soak the TVP in enough water to cover it. Chop all the vegetables and sauté them with the herbs and spices (including chilis) for 7 to 8 minutes, then add the TVP and cover the stew with enough water or bean stock to simmer the soy meat and vegetables. When they're nearly soft, add beans, salt, yeast extract or soy sauce, and tomato paste. Simmer for another 15 to 20 minutes, until thick, stirring often. Serve with brown rice and chopped cilantro leaves.

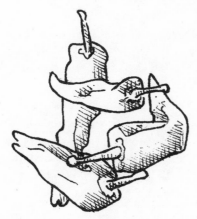

Savory Pies, Pasties, Fitters, and Crumbles

How to Make a Simple Pie Crust:
Makes a 9-inch pie crust

2¹/₂ C WHOLE WHEAT PASTRY FLOUR
¹/₂ t SALT
¹/₂ C OIL OR 6 OZ (1 ¹/₂ STICKS) BUTTER
3-4 T ICE WATER

Sift the flour and salt together and rub in the oil. Try not to handle the mixture more than necessary or the pastry will be tough. When the mixture is a fine crumbly texture add very cold water, a little at a time, until the pastry holds together. Roll out on a floured board.

9-INCH PIE CRUST

FILLING:

1 MEDIUM PARSNIP
1 MEDIUM CARROT
1 C PEELED AND HALVED BRUSSELS
  SPROUTS
A FEW LEAVES OF SPRING CABBAGE
  OR OTHER GREENS
¹/₂ t OREGANO
1 T FRESH PARSLEY, CHOPPED FINE
¹/₃ STICK BUTTER
¹/₂ t THYME
SALT AND PEPPER
¹/₂ C GRATED CHEDDAR CHEESE
2 TO 3 TOMATOES

Vegetable Pie
Serves 6

Steam the sprouts until soft (steam carrots and parsnips in a separate pan). Mash the carrots and parsnips together and add the herbs and seasoning. Mix in the greens and fill the pie crust with this mixture. Cover the top with a layer of grated cheese and slices of tomato and bake the pie for 20 minutes at 300°, until the top is golden and the pastry done. Adjust the vegetables according to your choice and the season.

CRUST:

¹/₃ **C** WHOLE WHEAT FLOUR

¹/₃ **C** WHEAT GERM

¹/₃ **C** SUNFLOWER OR SESAME SEEDS

2 OZ (¹/₂ STICK) BUTTER

PINCH OF SALT

¹/₃ **C** GRATED CHEDDAR CHEESE

FILLING:

2 lb FRESH SPINACH

¹/₂ **C** FINELY CHOPPED PARSLEY

2 OZ (¹/₂ STICK) BUTTER (FOR SAUTÉING)

I **C** GRATED CHEDDAR CHEESE

Spinach Pie
Serves 4

Combine all ingredients of crust together and rub in the butter with your fingertips to make a fine, crumbly mixture. Set it aside. Sauté the spinach and parsley in butter until cooked — 5 to 6 minutes will be long enough. Arrange half the spinach in a pie dish and cover with the grated cheese. Then another layer of spinach, and finally the crumble crust. Bake pie in a moderate oven until the top is golden.

2 C RED LENTILS
4 C WATER
2 OR 3 BAY LEAVES
1 t MILD **M**ADRAS CURRY POWDER
1 t SAGE
1 t THYME
¹/₂ t CELERY SEED
¹/₃ STICK BUTTER
1 C GRATED CHEDDAR CHEESE
1 T MUGI MISO
1 T TOMATO PASTE
1 t WHOLE GRAIN MUSTARD
ASSORTMENT OF SOFT VEGETABLES,
   E.G. FEW STICKS CELERY OR A
   SMALL CAULIFLOWER, A RED
   PEPPER, A FEW TOMATOES, OR
   ZUCCHINI
SALT AND PEPPER TO TASTE
1 ¹/₂ C BREAD CRUMBS TO THICKEN
SLICES OF RED PEPPER OR TOMATO TO
   DECORATE

Lentil Loaf

Serves 6-8

Cook the lentils in water with the bay leaves until soft and thick adding other herbs toward the end of the cooking. Lightly steam vegetables (except tomatoes). Mix the lentils, butter, cheese, miso, tomato paste, mustard, and vegetables together with a little salt and pepper and add bread crumbs until firm. Garnish with slices of tomato or pepper. Place the mixture in an oiled loaf pan and bake at 325° for 20 to 30 minutes until the top is browned and vegetables softened.

Carrot Pie
Serves 6

9-INCH PIE CRUST PRICKED WITH A
  FORK
4 TO 5 MEDIUM CARROTS
I T OIL (FOR SAUTÉING)
I C FINELY CHOPPED FRESH PARSLEY
5 OR 6 FRESH BASIL LEAVES, CHOPPED
SALT AND PEPPER TO TASTE
I T HONEY
FRESH COCONUT SLICES (OPTIONAL)

Chop and sauté the carrots for 5 minutes. Barely cover with water and simmer until tender. Meanwhile, brown the pie crust at 300° for 5 to 10 minutes. Mash or blend the carrots with parsley, basil, salt, pepper, and honey, and spread them over the pastry. Return to the oven and bake at 275° for 5 minutes more or until pie crust is golden. (Thicker, heavier pie crusts take longer.) Nice served with slices of fresh coconut.

Split Pea Fritters
Serves 4-5

I C DRY SPLIT PEAS (GREEN OR
  YELLOW), SOAKED OVERNIGHT
2 C WATER
2 BAY LEAVES
I C ROLLED OATS TO BIND
I T TOMATO PASTE
I t SAGE
I t PAPRIKA
¹/₃ T MADRAS CURRY POWDER
¹/₂ T MUGI MISO
SALT AND PEPPER TO TASTE
OIL FOR FRYING

Rinse the peas, cover them with water, and bring to a boil. Add the bay leaves and cook at least 30 minutes until thick. Let the peas cool and add small amount of rolled oats until the mixture is thick enough to form into balls. Add the tomato paste, sage, spices, and miso, adjust flavor with salt and pepper, and roll into egg-sized balls. Flatten them into patties and coat with oats. Heat some oil in a skillet or frying pan and fry the rissoles 2 or 3 minutes on each side.

Note:
To be served with cheese or parsley sauce, tomato catsup, and a crisp salad.

4 MEDIUM POTATOES, SLICED THIN

1 t OREGANO

1 t THYME

¹/₄ t ROSEMARY

1 OR 2 BAY LEAVES

SALT AND FRESHLY GROUND BLACK
PEPPER TO TASTE

¹/₂ C FRESH PARSLEY, CHOPPED FINE

2 TO 3 LARGE TOMATOES, SLICED

¹/₂ C CHOPPED BELL PEPPERS

¹/₂ C COOKED RED KIDNEY BEANS

¹/₂ C SLICED ZUCCHINI

1 C GRATED CHEDDAR CHEESE

1 C WATER IN WHICH **2 T** TOMATO
PASTE IS DISSOLVED

Potato Casserole
Serves 4

Use a deep casserole dish with a lid. Oil well and place a layer of potatoes in the bottom. Sprinkle with a layer of herbs and salt and pepper. Next scatter a layer of tomatoes, bell peppers, beans, and zucchini, and then a layer of cheese. Repeat until all potatoes are used, finishing with a layer of herbs. Pour in the water and cover the casserole tightly. Bake at 300° for 1 to 1 ¹/₂ hours.

2 C DICED BUTTERNUT SQUASH,
SKIN AND SEEDS REMOVED

1 ¹/₂ OZ (**¹/₃** STICK) BUTTER (FOR
SAUTÉING)

1 MEDIUM SIZED RED BELL PEPPER,
SEEDED AND CHOPPED

1 6-INCH LONG ZUCCHINI, SLICED
INTO ROUNDS

2 C SWEET CORN KERNELS

2 C SKINNED CHOPPED TOMATOES

¹/₂ T GROUND CORIANDER SEED

¹/₄ t GROUND GINGER

¹/₄ t GROUND ALLSPICE

¹/₂ t THYME

¹/₂ t DRY BASIL

SALT AND PEPPER TO TASTE

1 ¹/₂ C GRATED CHEDDAR CHEESE

Corn Squash Casserole
Serves 3

Sauté squash in butter for 5 minutes in a saucepan. Add bell pepper, zucchini, corn, and tomatoes with all seasonings and sauté 2 to 3 minutes longer. Transfer the mix to a deep oiled casserole dish and cover with grated cheese. Bake at 350° for 25 to 30 minutes. This casserole is delicious with a tangy side dish such as the Chunky Watercress Dip (p. 141).

9-INCH PIE CRUST (P. 66)

I **C** DRY ADZUKI BEANS BEANS,
   COOKED UNTIL SOFT (P. 23)

SALT AND BLACK PEPPER TO TASTE

I **T** MUGI MISO

2 **T** TOMATO PASTE

I **T** BUTTER

$^1/_2$ t THYME

$^1/_2$ t BASIL

$^1/_2$ t SAGE

$^1/_2$ t MARJORAM

$^1/_2$ t GROUND ANISE SEED

A FEW SESAME SEEDS

Adzuki Bean Pie

Serves 6

Make the pastry, roll it out, and place it in a shallow 8-inch pie dish, saving $^1/_3$ for the top (the recipe is for a 9-inch crust, so this will be enough). When the beans are ready, strain them and add salt, pepper, miso, tomato paste, butter, and herbs. Fill the pastry and cover with the remaining $^1/_3$ of the dough, rolled out to top the pie. Sprinkle with sesame seeds. Bake 25 to 30 minutes at 350° until the pastry is golden. Adzuki bean pie is great with potatoes, mashed, boiled, or fried. Save the stock from the beans and make some gravy, too.

2 **C** DRY GREEN LENTILS, SOAKED
   OVERNIGHT

6 **C** WATER

I t SAGE

3 BAY LEAVES

SALT AND PEPPER TO TASTE

I $^1/_2$ **C** GRATED CHEESE

2 OR 3 TOMATOES, SLICED

I TO I $^1/_2$ **C** SOFT ROLLED OATS
   (OPTIONAL)

Cheese and Lentil Bake

Serves 4-6

Cook lentils in the water with herbs for 1 to 1$^1/_2$ hours, until thick. Add salt and pepper towards the end of cooking. When they are thick, spread them into a baking tray, as you would a cake batter. If the lentils are not thick enough, use the rolled oats to thicken. Cover the top with a thick layer of grated cheese and slices of tomato. Place the tray in the oven and bake at 350° until cheese is toasted. This goes well with potato dishes, and with the Fried Plantain recipe (p. 120).

9-INCH PIE CRUST

FILLING:
4 OZ BUTTER (1 STICK)
1 ¹/₂ C SOFT ROLLED OATS
1 ¹/₂ C GRATED CHEDDAR CHEESE
SALT AND FRESHLY MILLED BLACK
  PEPPER TO TASTE
SLICES OF FRESH TOMATO
  (OPTIONAL)

Cheese and Oatmeal Pie
Serves 6

Melt the butter, stir in the oats
and cheese with seasoning, and
mix well together. Press the
mixture onto the pastry base
and top with slices of tomato.
Bake at 325° for 10 minutes.
Nice hot or cold.

3 C COOKED BULGUR WHEAT (P. 17)
1 C CRUSHED NUTS (WALNUTS,
  PEANUTS, BRAZILS, FILBERTS,
  CASHEWS, ALMONDS — ALL GOOD)
1 C LEFTOVER STEAMED VEGGIES,
  CHOPPED SMALL
¹/₂ C ALMOND OR PEANUT BUTTER
FLOUR FOR COATING
OIL FOR FRYING

Nutty Rissoles
(Vegetable Patties)
Makes 8 to 10 rissoles

Add nuts to the bulgur,
together with any leftover
vegetables, chopped small, and
bind ingredients together with
nut butter. Form into patties,
coat with flour and fry. These
freeze well and are good grilled
for barbecues.

Pasties (Turnovers)

Pasties are vegetable turnovers. The fillings can be varied according to your taste. First you must make some pie crust (p. 66) and roll it out and cut it into 6-inch squares. Now place a few spoonfuls of filling on the pastry square. Wet the edges of the pastry a little and fold it in half diagonally to form a triangle with the filling inside. Press or fold the edges together securely or seal with a pastry wheel. Bake them at 350° for 30 minutes or so until well-browned. Adzuki Bean Pie filling (p. 71) is nice in pasties. Try thick mixtures of split peas and vegetables as you would use in a stew. Pastie fillings should be extra spicy.

9-INCH PIE CRUST (P. 66),
  BUT QUADRUPLE THE RECIPE
2 LARGE POTATOES
I t OREGANO
I t THYME
2 T FRESH-CHOPPED PARSLEY
2 CARROTS
2 STICKS CELERY
2 SIX-INCH ZUCCHINI
3 TOMATOES
2 OZ (¹/₂ STICK) BUTTER (FOR
  SAUTÉING)
SALT AND PEPPER TO TASTE
I T THICK YEAST EXTRACT OR MUGI
  MISO
¹/₂ CAN (5 OZ) BRAISED WHEAT
  GLUTEN, CUT INTO SMALL PIECES

Potato Pasties
Makes about 16 large pasties

Boil or steam the potatoes, and meanwhile sauté the herbs and other vegetables in the butter, the harder ones first. When the vegetables are soft, add the potatoes, yeast extract and gluten, and continue cooking until the vegetables are well-mixed and the flavors nicely blended. Fill pastry squares. These can be frozen to use for summer picnics or trips.

Scouse

In the early 1960s, European children had hot lunches each day at school. The "school dinner" would arrive at mid-morning in giant steel canisters from some unknown dockside cookhouse and a penetrating smell of overcooked boiled cabbage would ooze through the classrooms and halls. One frequent school dinner was Scouse, a staple made from boiled mutton and potatoes, traditionally served with pickled red cabbage. Very poor people would have to leave out the mutton and then it would be called Blind Scouse. My mother, who considered herself middle class, called her Scouse "Irish Stew." Our family Scouse is now made with gluten, hence the name "One-Eyed Scouse." There's celery instead of onion in the recipe, and a few fresh herbs.

¹/₂ C TAMARI

13 C WATER

¹/₄ C SEITAN (GLUTEN) MIX
  (A COMMERCIAL MIX SUCH AS
  MADE BY ARROWHEAD MILLS)

¹/₂ TO ³/₄ C OIL

3 STICKS CELERY, CHOPPED

6 MEDIUM RED POTATOES

3 T EACH FRESH MINT AND BASIL,
  FINELY CHOPPED

4 T FRESH PARSLEY, FINELY CHOPPED

SALT AND GROUND BLACK PEPPER

One-eyed Scouse
Serves 4

Mix tamari with ¹/₂ C of the water and add to seitan mix in a large bowl. Knead well, then roll out 1-inch thick on a floured board and cut into ¹/₄-inch wide strips. Cut these 1 to 2 inches long and heat up the oil in a deep, heavy skillet. When a piece of seitan sizzles in the oil, lightly fry the seitan until golden. Set aside. Place the rest of the water in a large stockpot with a lid and add the celery and potatoes. Bring to a boil, add seitan, cover the pot, turn down, and simmer for 30 minutes. Add herbs, salt and pepper, and cook a little longer — just a minute or so, or if stew is still runny, it may need a little longer. Continue simmering until potatoes thicken the broth. Serve with pickles, especially red cabbage!

I 10-oz CUBE TOFU
¹/₂ C BREAD CRUMBS
¹/₃ C CRUSHED WALNUTS
2 T FINELY CHOPPED FRESH
  PARSLEY
SALT AND BLACK PEPPER TO TASTE
I T SOY SAUCE
FLOUR FOR COATING
OIL FOR DEEP FRYING
¹/₂ C CHEESE, ANY HARD VARIETY,
  GRATED

Savory Tofu Balls
Serves 4

Knead the tofu, bread crumbs, walnuts, parsley, salt and pepper, and soy sauce together and roll the mixture into balls. Coat them with flour and deep fry. Then place the balls in a shallow tray and cover them with grated cheese. Just before serving, brown them under the grill. Nice served with tomato sauce, especially an extra-spicy one.

3 SMALL CARROTS
2 OR 3 STICKS CELERY
I GREEN PEPPER
¹/₂ SMALL WHITE CABBAGE
3 T OIL (FOR SAUTÉING)
2 t MIXED DRIED HERBS (THYME,
  MARJORAM, SAGE, BASIL)
4 OR 5 SLICES WHOLE WHEAT BREAD
4 OZ PITTED OLIVES
SALT TO TASTE

Olive Vegetable Paté
Serves 4

Chop up the carrots, celery, pepper, and grate the cabbage. Sauté them beginning with the carrots and adding the other vegetables in the order listed, so that all soften together. Add the herbs with the cabbage. Meanwhile, soak the bread in water to soften it, and add it to the vegetables, mashing the mixture up in the pan. Add the olives and salt. The olives are usually very salty already, so not much is needed. Place the mixture in a buttered casserole dish and bake it at 200° for 30 to 40 minutes.

FILLING:

8 C CHOPPED IN-SEASON MIXED
    VEGETABLES
2 T MIXED DRIED HERBS (TRY BASIL,
    MARJORAM, OREGANO, SAGE,
    THYME)
¹/₂ T MILD MADRAS CURRY POWDER
2 ¹/₂ T OIL (FOR SAUTÉING)
I C COOKED BEANS, ANY VARIETY
2 ¹/₂ C WATER OR STOCK
2 T TOMATO PASTE
I T SOY SAUCE
SALT AND FRESHLY MILLED BLACK
    PEPPER TO TASTE

TOPPING:

I C WHOLE WHEAT FLOUR
I C BUCKWHEAT FLOUR
¹/₂ C OIL
PINCH OF SALT
¹/₄ C SUNFLOWER SEEDS

4 C WATER OR STOCK FROM
    COOKING RED KIDNEY OR ADZUKI
    BEANS
2 T TOMATO PASTE
2 CARROTS, CHOPPED
4 TO 5 T MISO PASTE, ANY VARIETY
I STICK CELERY
SALT AND PEPPER TO TASTE

Buckwheat Vegetable Crumble
Serves 6

In a medium-sized heavy saucepan, sauté vegetables, herbs and curry powder in oil for 3 to 4 minutes. Add the beans, water, tomato paste, and soy sauce. Bring to a boil, cover and simmer until vegetables are almost tender. Season to taste with salt and pepper. Transfer the contents of the saucepan to a large casserole dish. Now make the crumble topping. In a mixing bowl, rub the oil into the flours and salt until the mixture resembles bread crumbs. Stir in sunflower seeds. Scatter this mixture over the vegetables and bake uncovered at 350° for 30 minutes or until topping is browned. Serve with Miso Gravy (next recipe).

Miso Gravy
Serves 4-6

Simmer all ingredients together and, when carrots are tender, blend in an electric blender. Return to pan, re-heat and serve.

FOR THE CRUMBLE:

2 ¹/₂ C WHOLE WHEAT FLOUR

4 OZ (I STICK) BUTTER, OR

²/₃ C OIL

SALT

FILLING:

I MEDIUM CAULIFLOWER, BROKEN
INTO FLORETS

3 T FRESH CHOPPED PARSLEY

2 T OIL (FOR SAUTÉING)

¹/₂ C WATER

2 C COOKED OR CANNED CHICKPEAS
OR I C DRY CHICKPEAS, COOKED

2 T WHOLE WHEAT FLOUR MIXED TO
A PASTE WITH A LITTLE COLD
WATER

I C PLAIN YOGURT

SALT AND PEPPER TO TASTE

Chickpea and Cauliflower Crumble

Serves 4

Rub the butter into the flour and salt to make the crumble. Sauté the cauliflower with the parsley briefly in the oil. Add water and chickpeas. Cover and simmer for 2 to 3 minutes. Add flour paste and stir to thicken. Add yogurt and season to taste with salt and pepper. Turn into a glass casserole dish and sprinkle with the crumble mix. Bake at 300° for 15 to 20 minutes.

I C CASHEW NUT BUTTER

I C VEGETARIAN SAUSAGE MIX

I C ROLLED OATS

¹/₂ t MILD MADRAS CURRY POWDER

¹/₂ t CELERY SEED

I T MUGI MISO OR YEAST EXTRACT

I t THYME

SALT AND PEPPER TO TASTE

I t SAGE

I T TOMATO PASTE

I C BOILING WATER

Cashew Nut Roast

A delicious savory loaf, like a paté.
Serves 4-6

Mix nut butter with all other ingredients and pour boiling water into the bowl, mashing it into the mixture until a thick paste forms, and blending ingredients together well. Press the mixture into an oiled 5-inch x 9-inch loaf pan and bake at 300° for 15 to 20 minutes. This can be served with roast vegetables and gravy, or cut in slices when cold and served with salad.

2 ¹/₂ OZ (²/₃ STICK) BUTTER
2 T OIL
¹/₂ T SAGE
¹/₂ T DRY BASIL LEAF
1 ¹/₂ T MUGI MISO OR 1 T YEAST
   EXTRACT
2 ¹/₂ T TOMATO PASTE
¹/₂ T MILD MADRAS CURRY POWDER
5 C GRATED CARROT
3 ¹/₂ C GRATED CHEDDAR CHEESE
3 ¹/₂ C SOFT ROLLED OATS
SALT AND FRESHLY GROUND
BLACK PEPPER TO TASTE
SLICES OF FRESH TOMATO AND BELL
   PEPPER TO DECORATE

Carrot Bake
Serves 10

This is an incredibly useful recipe.
It is delicious hot or cold, keeps
well, is quick if you have a food
processor with a grating
attachment, and the ingredients are
available all year-round. One of my
perennial favorites. It freezes well;
make a batch of the mix and cook
half, saving the rest for the freezer.
Melt the oil and butter together in a
saucepan and stir in herbs, miso,
tomato paste, and curry powder,
smoothly blending all ingredients.
Combine the carrot, cheese, and
oats in a large mixing bowl, and stir
in the oil-butter mixture. Knead
until sticky, adding salt and pepper
to taste. Press 1-inch deep into oiled
baking dishes and decorate with
slices of tomato and pepper. Bake at
325° for about 20 minutes.

1 ¹/₂ OZ (¹/₃ STICK) BUTTER
¹/₃ C OIL
¹/₂ T MILD MADRAS CURRY POWDER
2 T MUGI MISO
2 T TOMATO PASTE
4 C GRATED CARROT
2 C BREAD CRUMBS
3 T MIXED DRIED HERBS
1 ¹/₂ C MINCED ROASTED UNSALTED
   PEANUTS
¹/₂ C NUTRITIONAL YEAST
SALT AND FRESHLY MILLED BLACK
   PEPPER TO TASTE

Carrot-Nut Bake
Serves 8 (freezes well)

Melt butter with oil, spices, miso,
and tomato paste. Mix carrots with
bread crumbs, herbs, peanuts, and
nutritional yeast and stir in the
melted butter mixture. Add salt
and pepper to taste. Knead to a
paste and press 1 ¹/₂ inches deep
into an oiled baking pan. Bake at
350° for 25 to 30 minutes.

1 BATCH **BLACKEYED PEAS IN HERB SAUCE** (P. 23)

1 **C** WATER

¹/₂ **C** FINELY CHOPPED CARROTS

1 STICK CELERY, FINELY CHOPPED

1 SMALL GREEN BELL PEPPER, FINELY CHOPPED

3 **C** VERMICELLI "NESTS," COOKED AS PER INSTRUCTIONS ON THE PACKAGE (THESE ARE AVAILABLE FROM GOOD **I**TALIAN DELIS)

1 **C** GRATED CHEDDAR CHEESE

Blackeyed Peas with Vermicelli
Serves 5-6

Heat water and simmer the vegetables gently in a covered pot until tender, adding pepper 5 minutes after carrot and celery. Combine all ingredients except cheese (including the water from cooking the vegetables) and turn into a shallow casserole dish. Sprinkle with cheese and bake at 275° for 15 to 20 minutes.

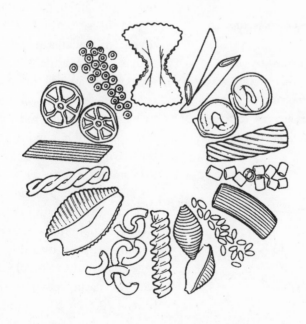

4 LARGE, 6 MEDIUM, OR 8 SMALL
   POTATOES
1 ¹/₂ C BRUSSELS SPROUTS, WITH
   OUTER LEAVES REMOVED, HALVED
2 MEDIUM CARROTS, SLICED
1 MEDIUM PARSNIP, CHOPPED
2 STICKS CELERY, SLICED
1 SMALL BEET, CHOPPED, WITH
   LEAVES
2 C SHREDDED SPINACH
1 BELL PEPPER, CHOPPED
1 10 OZ CAN MOCK DUCK
   (AVAILABLE IN CHINESE STORE) OR
   OTHER BRAND OF CANNED
   GLUTEN
¹/₂ C FRESH PARSLEY, FINELY
   CHOPPED
¹/₂ C CHEDDAR CHEESE, GRATED
1 t THYME
1 t GROUND CORIANDER SEED
SALT AND FRESHLY MILLED BLACK
   PEPPER TO TASTE
A LITTLE MILK, BUTTER, YOGURT,
   SOUR CREAM, OR BUTTERMILK

Cottage Pie
Serves 5-6

Scrub and cut potatoes and put
them into a large pot with a lid.
Cover with cold water, bring to
a boil, and boil the potatoes
until soft. Put the rest of the
vegetables in a large colander
or vegetable steamer, and place
this over the potatoes. Put the
lid on the pot and steam the
vegetables until tender while
the potatoes boil. Transfer the
vegetables (not the potatoes) to
a large oiled casserole dish and
mix in the gluten, parsley, and
grated cheese. Sprinkle with
thyme, coriander, salt and
pepper, and set aside. When
the potatoes are soft, drain and
cool them and then peel them
by hand (or simply prod with a
fork while still hot and peel off
the scarred or rough areas of
skin and leave the rest). Mash
the potatoes with a little milk
and butter (or use sour cream,
yogurt, or buttermilk) and add
salt and pepper. Cover the
vegetables in the casserole dish
with the mashed potatoes and
bake at 200° for 20-30 minutes
to brown the surface a little.
Serve with Parsley Sauce
(p. 96) or catsup.

BATTER:

1 **C** WHITE FLOUR OR CHICKPEA
(GARBANZO) FLOUR

1 TO 1 1/4 **C** MILK

1/2 t SALT

1/2 t BAKING POWDER

VEGETABLE MARINADE:

USE AN HERBED VINEGAR OR A MILD
SOY SAUCE

OIL (FOR DEEP FRYING)

Tempura

A delightful and exotic addition to a plain meal. You can make as much as you need and if batter is left over it keeps well in the refrigerator.

If you are using hard vegetables, steam them lightly first, until barely tender. Marinate the vegetables for 1 hour. Mix the batter. Dip the fruit or vegetable pieces into the batter and deep fry. Try with cauliflower florets, Jerusalem artichoke slices, Brussels sprouts, parsnip chunks, beet pieces, or carrot slices, all steamed, or with pieces of zucchini or bell pepper, or with sprigs of fresh parsley or cilantro, or chunks of firm tofu. Also try with pieces of banana, unmarinated.

Chapter 6

Soups

2 PARSNIPS

2 CARROTS

I SMALL TURNIP OR RUTABAGA

2 STICKS CELERY

A FEW BAY LEAVES

I $^1/_2$ **t** THYME

$^1/_2$ **t** ROSEMARY

I t GROUND CORIANDER

I t MARJORAM

$^1/_4$ **t** MACE

3 T OIL (FOR SAUTÉING)

4 $^1/_2$ **C** WATER

I SPRING CABBAGE OR OTHER
    DARK GREENS

ROUX:

2 OZ ($^1/_2$ STICK) BUTTER

3 T FLOUR (WHITE OR WHOLE
    WHEAT)

2 $^1/_2$ **C** MILK

Vegetable Soup
Serves 4-6

Chop all the vegetables finely (the greens a bit bigger). In a large saucepan sauté all the vegetables (except the greens) with the herbs for 2 to 3 minutes. Now cover them with water and bring to a boil. Add the greens, cover the pan, and simmer the vegetables for about 15 minutes, or until quite tender.

Meanwhile, make the roux. Melt the butter in a saucepan and when melted add the flour, stirring it in and cooking gently for a few minutes. Remove the pan from the heat and add a little water, mixing it thoroughly with the flour and butter (a wire whisk is helpful for this). Now add the milk a little at a time, and continue stirring, or the roux may go lumpy. When the flour and milk are thoroughly blended, return pan to the heat and bring to a simmer, stirring constantly. If you don't, the flour sinks to the bottom and cooks and then your sauce gets lumpy. If it does this, you will have to purée it, but if you stir all the time, it won't. Simmer the sauce until nicely thick — about a minute.

As soon as the vegetables are cooked, pour a little of their stock into the sauce and blend, then return all to the vegetable pan and blend the sauce and vegetables together. Add seasoning. It is nice to serve this soup with lots of freshly chopped parsley. For a more substantial meal, you can add roasted buckwheat to the vegetables when they're about half done and this adds a delicious flavor.

1 t OREGANO
2 t THYME
1 t SAGE
1 t MARJORAM
2 BAY LEAVES
¹/₄ STICK BUTTER (FOR SAUTÉING)
2 POTATOES, CHOPPED
2 CARROTS, PEELED AND SLICED
1 GREEN PEPPER
1 STICK CELERY, CHOPPED
1 PARSNIP, SLICED
2 C GREENS, CHOPPED FINE
5 C WATER OR VEGETABLE STOCK
2 C MILK
SALT AND PEPPER TO TASTE

Cream of Vegetable Soup
Serves 6-8

In a deep saucepan, sauté herbs with all the vegetables in the butter and add water or stock. Bring to a boil, turn down heat, cover the pan, and simmer for 20 minutes or until the vegetables are tender. Take out the bay leaf, purée the stock and vegetables with milk in a blender (in batches), and reheat. Season and serve piping hot, garnished with fresh parsley.

6 C FRESH SPINACH, SHREDDED
¹/₂ C WATER
2 OZ (¹/₂ STICK) BUTTER
1 C MILK
SALT AND PEPPER TO TASTE

Spinach Soup
Deep green, rich, and very tasty.
Serves 2-3

Cook spinach in water in a covered saucepan for 6 to 8 minutes, then blend to a purée in a blender with the cooking water. Reheat with butter and milk, but do not boil. When scalding hot, add seasoning and serve.

4 C PEELED CHOPPED TOMATOES

I BAY LEAF

I t OREGANO

I t BASIL

I ^{1}/$_2$ OZ (^{1}/$_3$ STICK) BUTTER

2 ^{1}/$_2$ C WATER

6 T TOMATO PASTE

SALT AND PEPPER TO TASTE

I T CORNSTARCH

^{1}/$_2$ C MILK

^{1}/$_2$ t MARJORAM

Tomato Soup
Serves 4

Sauté the tomatoes with the herbs, except marjoram, in the butter. When they are soft, add all the liquid and bring it to a boil, adding the tomato paste and the salt and pepper. Mix the cornstarch with a little cold water. When the soup is simmering, add the cornstarch mixture and stir until thick. Add milk and marjoram and re-heat. Taste it to adjust the seasoning. You could try adding some thick yogurt or sour cream to this soup just before serving (don't stir it in) which is delicious.

4 C RED POTATOES DICED INTO

  ^{1}/$_2$-INCH CUBES

4 C WATER

^{1}/$_2$ t ROSEMARY

I t SAGE

^{1}/$_4$ t CELERY SEED

I OZ (^{1}/$_4$ STICK) BUTTER

I C MILK

^{1}/$_2$ t PAPRIKA

SALT AND FRESHLY MILLED

  BLACK PEPPER TO TASTE

Creamed Potato Soup
Serves 4

Boil the potatoes in the 4 C water until soft, and then purée them with the cooking water in an electric blender. Return to the pan and re-heat, adding all other ingredients. Simmer gently for 3 to 4 minutes and serve.

2 CUCUMBERS (6 TO 8 INCHES LONG), PEELED
2 ¹/₂ C MILK
2 C SWEET CORN KERNELS
SALT AND FRESHLY MILLED BLACK PEPPER

Chilled Cucumber Soup
Serves 3-4

Blend all ingredients and chill. Take care adding the salt; salty flavors are enhanced when food is chilled.

2 C DRY RED LENTILS
6 C WATER
2 BAY LEAVES
¹/₄ t SAVORY HERB
1 OZ (¹/₄ STICK) BUTTER
5 TO 6 LEAVES FRESH SWEET BASIL, FINELY SHREDDED (IF YOU CAN'T GET FRESH BASIL, USE 2T FRESH PARSLEY LEAVES, CHOPPED FINE)
SALT AND FRESHLY MILLED BLACK PEPPER

Lentil Soup
Serves 4-6

Soak the lentils for 1 hour, rinse and drain. In a large stockpot bring them to a boil with the water and bay leaves and simmer for 30 minutes, adding savory after 15 minutes. Add the butter and basil, cook 1 minute longer, and add salt and pepper. Serve. You can also add a few chopped fresh vegetables to this soup with the savory. Nice ones are celery, tomatoes, celeriac, and bell peppers.

4 **C** PARSNIPS, SCRUBBED BUT NOT
   PEELED, DICED INTO ¹/₂-INCH CUBES
2 ¹/₂ **C** WATER
2 ¹/₂ **C** MILK
1 OZ (¹/₄ STICK) BUTTER
¹/₂ t THYME
¹/₂ t MARJORAM
¹/₄ t SAGE
PINCH OF MACE

Parsnip Soup
Serves 4

Simmer the parsnips in water
for 10 to 15 minutes until soft.
Transfer the parsnips and
cooking water to a blender and
blend to a purée. Return to pan
and reheat with all other
ingredients, and serve.

3 TO 4 **C** CUT MIXED ROOT
   VEGETABLES
2 t MIXED DRIED HERBS
2 **T** OIL
6 **C** WATER
1 **C** YOUNG NETTLE TIPS
SALT AND FRESHLY MILLED BLACK
   PEPPER TO TASTE

Nettle Soup
Serves 4-6

We used to gather the young
tender nettle tops each spring
to use in vegetable broths. If
grasped very firmly they don't
sting, a fact I discovered one
day when I had lost my
gardening glove. The flavor is
not to everybody's taste, but
worth a try, and after all, free.
Sauté root vegetables and herbs
in the oil for 4 to 5 minutes,
cover with water, and bring to
a boil. Add nettles. Simmer
covered until roots are tender.
Season and serve.

4 **C** DICED RED POTATOES (¹/₂-INCH
  CUBES)
4 **C** WATER (FOR POTATOES)
2 STICKS CELERY, CHOPPED SMALL
1 OZ (¹/₄ STICK) BUTTER
2¹/₂ **T** FRESH PARSLEY, CHOPPED FINE
1¹/₂ **T** FRESH MINT, CHOPPED FINE
1 **C** WATER FOR CELERY
1 **C** LIGHT CREAM
SALT AND FRESHLY MILLED BLACK
  PEPPER

Potato and Celery Soup
Serves 4-6

Boil potatoes in water until soft and blend them in an electric blender with the cooking water until smooth. In a separate pan, sauté the celery in the butter for 3 to 4 minutes, cover with water and simmer gently for 20 minutes until tender. Add puréed potatoes to the celery with the other ingredients and reheat to not quite boiling. Serve.

2¹/₂ **C** PRE-SOAKED SPLIT PEAS,
  YELLOW OR GREEN (1 **C** DRY)
1 t SAGE
2 TO 3 BAY LEAVES
4 PINTS WATER OR STOCK
  SALT AND BLACK PEPPER
1 t MARJORAM, THYME, POWDERED
  GINGER, BASIL, OR MACE

Split Pea Soup
Serves 3-4

Rinse the peas and bring them to a boil with the herbs and stock. Simmer 30 minutes, adding more water when necessary. You can make this soup really thick if you like, but stir often. Add any vegetables you might choose after about 20 minutes. Try celery, carrots, parsnips, turnips, rutabaga, greens, potatoes, tomatoes, green or red peppers. Have fun experimenting with different combinations of herbs and vegetables. This is a very basic and versatile recipe.

3 **C** RED POTATOES, PEELED AND
   DICED SMALL

1 1/2 OZ (1/3 STICK) BUTTER

1/4 t TURMERIC

1 1/2 t CORIANDER POWDER

1/2 t NUTMEG

1/4 MACE

1 t PAPRIKA

1/2 t GINGER POWDER

3 BAY LEAVES

2 **C** SWEET CORN KERNELS

6 **C** WATER

SALT AND PEPPER TO TASTE

FRESH CHOPPED PARSLEY OR
   CILANTRO FOR GARNISH

Yellow Corn and Potato Soup
Serves 4-6

Sauté potatoes and spices in butter briefly in a heavy stockpot or saucepan. Add corn and water, cover pot and simmer slowly for 25 minutes. Serve with fresh chopped parsley or cilantro.

2 t PAPRIKA

1 t TURMERIC

DASH OF CINNAMON

1 **C** DICED CELERY

1 SMALL BUNCH PARSLEY

1 t SALT

3 TO 4 **T** OLIVE OIL

2 **C** STEAMED SQUASH
   (AND THEIR COOKING WATER)

1 1/2 **C** COOKED CHICKPEAS
   (AND THEIR COOKING WATER)

3 1/2 **C** CHOPPED TOMATOES

1 BUNCH KALE, CHOPPED

Chickpea and Butternut Squash Soup
Serves 4-6

Sauté spices, celery, parsley and salt in oil. Add the rest of the ingredients with enough water to cover and give a soup consistency. Cook gently for 30 minutes in a covered stockpot.

2 SMALL CARROTS

3 LEAVES FROM A SPRING CABBAGE
  OR OTHER DARK GREENS

1 STICK CELERY

6 C WATER

1/2 t THYME

1 t OREGANO

3 T MUGI MISO

2 T TOMATO PASTE

SALT AND FRESHLY MILLED BLACK
  PEPPER TO TASTE

Miso and Vegetable Soup
Serves 4

Simple, quick and very tasty. Good in a thermos flask for a hot lunch on a cold day — can be made up in the morning.

Chop vegetables and cover with water in a saucepan. Add the thyme and oregano. Bring to a boil and add the miso and tomato paste. Lower heat, cover, and simmer 10 to 15 minutes until vegetables are tender. Season with salt and pepper.

1 SMALL HEAD OF CELERY

2 OZ (1/2 STICK) BUTTER
  (FOR SAUTÉING)

1 t GROUND CORIANDER SEED

1 t MARJORAM

2 BAY LEAVES

1 C WATER

3 C MILK

3 T CORNSTARCH, DISSOLVED IN A
  LITTLE COLD WATER

SALT AND FRESHLY MILLED BLACK
  PEPPER TO TASTE

Cream of Celery Soup
Serves 4

Chop the celery finely and sauté it in the butter with herbs and coriander for 3 minutes. Add the water, bring to a boil, cover, and simmer 15 to 20 minutes until the celery is soft. Add the milk and re-heat until nearly boiling. Stir in the cornstarch, stirring constantly, and continue stirring until the soup thickens. Season with salt and pepper and serve.

Chapter 7

Sauces

There are several ways to make a sauce, but some methods are very complicated, so in this book we only use two methods. Whole wheat flour can be used to thicken some sauces (cheese sauce for instance), but when a very subtle flavor is required, whole wheat flour tends to drown the taste. For these more delicate sauces, cornstarch can be used. If you don't like using refined starches, use arrowroot. When using whole wheat flour, follow Method 1.

Method 1: The Roux

2 T BUTTER OR OIL
2 T WHOLE WHEAT FLOUR
2 C MILK
SALT

Melt the butter in a heavy saucepan and stir in the flour. Cook this mixture over a gentle flame for a minute or two. Remove from the heat. Blend in the milk, very gradually, a little at a time (a wire whisk helps with this). It will sizzle and boil. If you add it all at once or can't blend it properly, the sauce will be lumpy. When all the milk is added and the mixture is very smooth, return it to the heat and gently bring it to a simmer. Ṣtir it constantly. Simmer it for 3 to 4 minutes until it is nice and thick. The sauce is now ready for the flavoring to be added.

Cheese Sauce
Serves 3-4

Make a roux (Method 1). Stir in some grated cheese — the more cheese, the stronger the sauce — and some paprika. Use it for macaroni, rice, fritters, vegetables, etc. 2 C grated sharp cheddar makes a tasty but mild sauce.

Tahini Sauce
Serves 3-4

Make a roux (Method 1). Stir in 1/2 C tahini and continue cooking the sauce for a few minutes. Goes well with wheat grain.

TRY:

I t DRIED SAGE

I t DRIED THYME

I t DRIED PARSLEY

Herb Sauce
Serves 3-4

Make a roux (Method 1). Sauté a selection of your favorite herbs together with the flour and butter before adding milk.

Peanut Butter Sauce
Serves 3-4

Make a roux (Method 1). Stir in 1/2 C peanut butter. You may need to use a blender to achieve a smooth texture.

Method 2: Basic Sauce

This is very simple. Heat 2 ¹/₂ C milk and 2 oz (¹/₂ stick) butter in a saucepan. When almost boiling, lower heat and stir in 2 ¹/₂ T cornstarch dissolved in a little cold water. Stir constantly until the cornstarch thickens the milk. Add salt and other ingredients.

Nutmeg Sauce
Serves 4

To the basic sauce (Method 2) add ¹/₂ t grated nutmeg before thickening. Goes well with steamed cauliflower, sautéed cabbage, and sweet root vegetables such as Jerusalem artichokes, sweet potatoes, and parsnips.

Parsley Sauce
Serves 4

Make a basic sauce (Method 2). In a blender, blend half the milk with 1 ¹/₂ to 2 C coarsely chopped fresh parsley and add to the remainder of the milk in the saucepan. Heat up and thicken.

Chestnut Sauce
Serves 4

To the basic sauce (Method 2) add 1 C boiled, peeled, and halved chestnuts, with a pinch of mace and garam masala.

Caper Sauce
Serves 4

Stir 2 to 3 T capers into the basic sauce (Method 2) after thickening.

4 TO 5 LARGE TOMATOES, SKINNED
1 ½ OZ (⅓ STICK) BUTTER (FOR SAUTÉING)
1 t BASIL
1 t OREGANO
1 ½ C WATER
1 SMALL CAN TOMATO PASTE
SALT AND PEPPER TO TASTE
2 T CORNSTARCH, DISSOLVED IN A LITTLE COLD WATER

Tomato Sauce
Serves 4-5

According to cost and season, you can choose to make this with fresh tomatoes or mostly tomato paste. Here is a recipe that compromises.

Chop the tomatoes and sauté them in the butter with the herbs until they cook down. Add the liquid, tomato paste, and seasoning and heat it all up. Add cornstarch. Taste it to adjust the seasoning. This sauce goes with fritters and rissoles of all kinds, stuffed vegetables, plain grains, and lots of other things.

¹/₄ **C** BUTTER

¹/₄ **C** BLANCHED, FINELY CHOPPED
ALMONDS, CASHEWS, BRAZILS,
SUNFLOWER SEEDS, ETC.

Buttered Nut Sauce
Serves 2

Melt butter over a low heat and
when it begins to brown, add
nuts, stirring until hot. Add a
little salt and pour over grains
or vegetables.

¹/₂ **T** GRATED FRESH GINGER ROOT

I RED CHILI, FRESH OR DRIED, WITH
SEEDS FOR EXTRA HOT FLAVOR

¹/₂ **t** ASAFETIDA (HING) (P. 196)

I T OIL

3 C WATER

I C CRUSHED ROASTED PEANUTS

2 T SOY SAUCE

¹/₂ **C** PEANUT BUTTER, SMOOTH OR
CRUNCHY

SALT TO TASTE

Hot Peanut Sauce
Serves 4-6

Sauté spices in oil for 1 to 2
minutes and add water, nuts,
and soy sauce. Simmer gently
for 20 minutes, stirring
regularly. Add peanut butter
and cook a further 5 minutes,
stirring constantly. Add salt to
taste. Pour over grains and
vegetables.

Chapter 8

International Dishes

Recipes from India

6 **C** DICED OR CHOPPED MIXED
   VEGETABLES, INCLUDING CARROTS,
   PARSNIPS, CAULIFLOWER, GREENS,
   POTATO, OKRA, GREEN PEPPERS,
   BRUSSELS SPROUTS, ZUCCHINI,
   EGGPLANT, TOMATOES
2 **t** TURMERIC
4 **t** GROUND CUMIN SEED
   (MUST BE REALLY FRESH)
2 **t** GARAM MASALA (P. 199)
2 **t** CHILI POWDER
3 **T** OIL (FOR SAUTÉING)
3 **T** LEMON JUICE
1 **T** PEANUT BUTTER
4 **T** TOMATO PASTE
3 TO 4 **T** FLOUR, DISSOLVED IN A
   LITTLE COLD WATER
SALT TO TASTE

Bombay Yellow Curry
Serves 4

Sauté the vegetables and spices together for 5 minutes, omitting softer vegetables. Cover with water to the top of the vegetables, adding the softer vegetables, lemon juice, peanut butter, and tomato paste. Simmer for 15 to 20 minutes, then add flour, stirring constantly. Stir until thick, season with salt and serve.

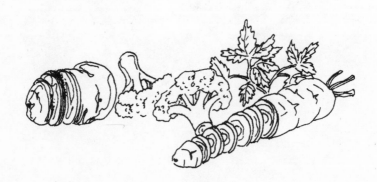

1 lb (ABOUT 11 TO 12 C)
SHREDDED FRESH SPINACH
2/3 C UNSALTED RAW CASHEWS
1 t GARAM MASALA (P. 199)
1 t GRATED FRESH GINGER ROOT
3 SMALL ZUCCHINI, THINLY SLICED
1/2 t EACH: WHOLE FENUGREEK,
   CORIANDER, AND CUMIN SEED
1 T OIL
1/8 t TURMERIC
PINCH OF POWDERED CARDAMOM SEED
SPRINKLE OF LIME JUICE

Spinach Cashew Curry
Serves 3-4

Sauté all ingredients together for 7 to 10 minutes and serve with a sprinkle of lime juice.

2 TO 3 T OIL (FOR SAUTÉING)
1 SMALL ROOT FRESH GINGER
   (1/2 OZ), SLICED THINLY
1/4 t WHOLE BLACK PEPPERCORNS
1/2 t WHOLE CUMIN SEEDS
1/2 t WHOLE CORIANDER SEEDS
2 OR 3 WHOLE GREEN CHILIS,
   CHOPPED FINE
8 C MIXED VEGETABLES, FINELY
   CHOPPED (CARROTS, POTATOES, ETC.)
2 CUPS WATER
1 lb CAN TOMATOES
SALT TO TASTE

Hot Vegetable Curry
Serves 6

Heat oil in a large skillet or frying pan with a lid. Sauté spices for a minute, then add vegetables (except tomatoes), stirring constantly. Sauté for several minutes, then add water. Add the tomatoes, cover, and simmer slowly until vegetables are tender. If you want to thicken the curry, add 1 to 2 T cornstarch or arrowroot, mixed to a paste with a little water, at the end of cooking.

**1 BATCH GRAM FLOUR PANCAKE
   BATTER (P. 25)**
OIL FOR DEEP-FRYING

Pakora
Serves 6-8

Drop teaspoonfuls of batter
into hot oil and deep-fry
several at a time, to make very
tasty crispy balls. They can be
served with curry or eaten on
their own.

2 C DRY GREEN LENTILS
1 1/2 OZ (1/3 STICK) BUTTER
1/2 t GROUND GINGER
1/2 t TURMERIC
1 t GROUND CUMIN SEED
1 1/2 t GROUND CORIANDER SEED
SALT TO TASTE

Green Lentil Dal
Serves 4-6

Soak and then cook the lentils
to a smooth, thick consistency.
Add butter and spices. Simmer
5 minutes, stirring constantly.
Season with salt.

2 ½ C PRE-SOAKED MUNG BEANS
   (I C DRY)
2 OZ. BUTTER
¼ t TURMERIC
I t GROUND CUMIN SEED
SALT AND PEPPER
I t GROUND CORIANDER SEEDS
I t GRATED FRESH GINGER ROOT
⅛ t CHILI POWDER

Mung Bean Dal
Serves 4-6

Wash, sort, and cook mung beans in 2 ½ C water in a pressure cooker for 25 minutes, or with 4 C water in a saucepan until soft and thick, stirring regularly. Add butter and spices and simmer 5 minutes longer. Season and serve.

Panir (Soft Indian Cheese)
This is a delicious cheese served with vegetables in a spicy sauce.

Bring 2 pints fresh milk to a boil and add the juice of a lemon. Turn off the heat and let it sit for a few moments — it will curdle. Bring it back to a boil again and then leave it to cool. When it is lukewarm, pour it into a clean piece of cheesecloth or muslin and leave to drip. (Do not squeeze the bag, or your cheese will be tacky.) When firm, knead in a little salt. This cheese is generally cubed and fried in butter and then added to curried vegetables. (It's really delicious prepared this way.) The whey which drains from the cheese can be used in baking, for bread and scones.

RAITA

Raita is a chilled preparation of yogurt with fruits or vegetables. It is delicately spiced and has a cooling effect when eaten with a hot curry.

I t SALT
¹/₂ t PEPPER
I t CUMIN SEEDS, ROASTED
¹/₂ T OIL
¹/₂ t BLACK MUSTARD SEEDS
2 C YOGURT
5 C FINELY CHOPPED COOKED
   POTATOES

Alu Raita
Serves 6

Sauté spices in oil in a small skillet for 1 to 2 minutes, until mustard seeds pop. Mix all ingredients, chill and serve.

2 C PLAIN YOGURT
2 C SLICED BANANAS
I t CUMIN SEEDS, ROASTED
A PINCH EACH OF CORIANDER AND
   GROUND CARDAMOM
PINCH OF SALT

Banana Raita
Serves 3-4

Mix, chill and serve. The cumin seeds can be roasted beforehand in a dry skillet to release their flavor.

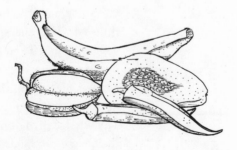

2 C YOGURT

2 C GRATED PEELED CUCUMBER

¹/₂ t CUMIN SEEDS, ROASTED

¹/₄ t WHOLE NIGELLA SEED **(P. 200)**

SALT TO TASTE

Cucumber Raita
Serves 2-3

Mix, chill and serve.

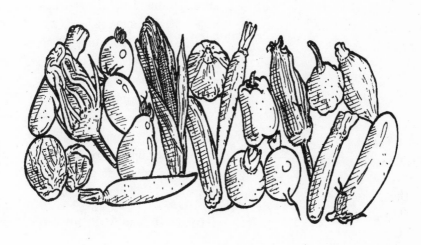

2 C MILK
3/4 C SUGAR
8 OZ (2 STICKS) BUTTER
2 1/4 C REFINED SEMOLINA
(CREAM OF WHEAT®)
1/2 C RAISINS (GOLDEN RAISINS,
OR SULTANAS, ARE TRADITIONAL)
1/2 C CHOPPED ALMONDS
DESICCATED COCONUT TO ROLL IN

Indian Halvah
Serves 6-8 (keeps well in refrigerator)

Heat the milk gently and add the sugar. Stir from time to time while heating, so the sugar dissolves. Meanwhile, melt the butter in another large pan and when liquid, add the semolina. Stir well so that the semolina absorbs the butter and cooks over the heat. Be careful not to burn it. Cook for about 5 minutes. When the milk is boiling, remove the semolina/butter from the heat and pour the milk on to it slowly, meanwhile stirring the mixture. Now return to the heat, stirring well for a minute or two until all ingredients are thoroughly cooked together. Remove from heat, add fruit and nuts. Roll up tablespoons of the mixture into small balls and roll them in coconut. Leave them to cool.

I STICK BUTTER
I C POWDERED SUGAR
I C BABY MILK POWDER
(NOT SOY-BASED)

Triipti's Indian Milk Sweets
Serves 6-8

With your warm hands, squeeze the butter until it is very soft. Now squeeze the sugar and milk powder into the butter. Keep kneading the mixture until it is soft, creamy, and well- blended. Pinch off small pieces and roll them into balls. That's all. You can add various other ingredients to this mixture, for instance, chopped nuts. It's the additives in the infant formula that give these sweets their characteristic flavor. If you prefer, use regular whole milk powder.

Recipes from the Far East

$^1/_2$ **C** CARROTS, DICED SMALL

$^1/_2$ **C** CELERY, DICED FINELY

2-3 C SHREDDED **C**HINESE CABBAGE
  OR BOK CHOY

$^1/_2$ **C** SUGAR SNAP PEAS OR OTHER
  FRESH OR FROZEN BEANS

$^1/_2$ **C** GREEN OR RED PEPPERS, CHOPPED

SMALL CAN BAMBOO SHOOTS

I C BEAN SPROUTS

$^1/_2$ **C** DICED CUCUMBER

$^1/_4$ **C** CASHEW OR CHOPPED **B**RAZIL
  NUTS

I CAN BABY CORN SPEARS

ABOUT $^1/_2$ **C** OIL (FOR STIR-FRYING)

MARINADE:

I C SOY SAUCE

I t CHILI POWDER

2 t GRATED FRESH GINGER ROOT

2 t GROUND CORIANDER POWDER

Vegetable Chop Suey
Serves 6

Any soft or firm vegetables (but not starchy) can be used in chop suey, e.g. string beans, peas, etc. (Be careful with leafy vegetables, as they burn easily.) The recipe below is only one example. Leftover cooked beans can also be added. The mixture should be very colorful.

Marinate vegetables for at least an hour before cooking. Stir-fry vegetables quickly in hot oil, preferably using a wok (Chinese round-bottomed frying pan). Use an oil that can heat to high temperatures without chemical change (peanut or sesame oil). Use plenty of oil to prevent burning (allow oil to be at least 1 inch deep in the deepest part of the wok). Fry hard vegetables for 5 to 6 minutes, then add softer vegetables like fresh beans, bell peppers, and cabbage or bok choy, and fry 3 minutes more, adding cucumber, nuts, and bean sprouts only $^1/_2$ minute before the end. Sprinkle with soy sauce and serve with rice or noodles, and tofu dishes. Save the marinade to use as a dip.

I T BAKER'S YEAST

$^1/_2$ T SUGAR OR HONEY

$^1/_4$ C WARM WATER

2 $^1/_4$ C WHITE FLOUR, UNBLEACHED

1 $^1/_4$ T OIL

$^1/_4$ t SALT

$^1/_2$ TO $^3/_4$ C WARM MILK

<u>SWEET FILLING:</u>

MIX TOGETHER:

$^2/_3$ C SESAME SEEDS, COARSELY
   GROUND

$^1/_3$ C DESICCATED COCONUT

$^1/_2$ t GROUND ALLSPICE

$^1/_2$ t GINGER POWDER

$^1/_4$ t EACH OF FINELY GROUND
   CLOVES AND FENNEL SEEDS

3 T HONEY

2 T SUGAR

<u>SAVORY FILLING:</u>

MIX TOGETHER:

1 $^1/_3$ C SOFT COOKED ADZUKI BEANS
   (P. 23)

2 t DRIED TARRAGON LEAF

$^1/_2$ t SALT

$^1/_2$ t EACH OF FINELY GROUND STAR
   ANISE AND FENNEL SEED

$^1/_2$ OZ ($^1/_8$ STICK) BUTTER

PINCH OF TURMERIC

Dim Sum
Makes nine 4-inch dumplings

These are gorgeous little filled yeast dumplings with sweet or savory fillings, cooked by steaming.

In a small bowl, mix yeast with sugar and warm water and set in a warm place for 15 minutes. Warm flour in a large mixing bowl. Combine flour, oil, and salt and pour in yeast mixture, which should be frothy. Add milk. Knead for at least 10 minutes, (with a food processor you can do this using the dough hook), until the dough is springy and elastic. It should not be sticky when ready. If it is still sticky after lots of kneading, add a little more flour. Set in a warm place, covered with a towel, for 20 minutes. Roll dough out on a well-floured surface to an 18-inch x 18-inch square. (Yes, it will stretch this far!) Cut into nine 6-inch squares.

Place a small amount of sweet or savory filling in the center of each. Wet the edges of the squares and pinch them together around the filling. Turn, shape into neat circles, and place the dumplings side by side on a vegetable steaming rack or in a large colander. Steam for a $^1/_2$ hour or until dough is cooked. Serve immediately. They can also be frozen when still raw.

2 **C** SUGAR SNAP PEAS

I SMALL BELL PEPPER, SEEDED
   AND FINELY CHOPPED

2 **T** OIL (FOR SAUTÉING)

¹/₂ **C** SLICED WATER CHESTNUTS

2 **t** GRATED FRESH GINGER ROOT

¹/₈ **t** CHILI POWDER

4 **C** WATER OR VEGETABLE STOCK

2 **t** HONEY

2 **T** CIDER VINEGAR

I **T** SOY SAUCE

Hot and Sour Pea Soup

Serves 6

Sauté the peas and bell pepper in the oil until bright green. Remove from oil and sauté the water chestnuts, ginger, and chili powder briefly. Cover with water and add honey, vinegar, and soy sauce. Bring to a boil and re-add vegetables. Season to taste with salt and pepper and serve.

3 **T** FRESH PARSLEY, FINELY CHOPPED

2 BAY LEAVES

¹/₂ **t** PAPRIKA

I **T** OIL (FOR SAUTÉING)

5 **C** WATER

I 10-OZ CAN GLUTEN

2 **T** SOY SAUCE

I STICK CELERY

I BUNCH CELLOPHANE NOODLES
   (I INCH IN DIAMETER)

2 **C** SNOW PEAS

I JALAPENO PEPPER, CHOPPED FINE
   WITHOUT THE SEEDS

²/₃ **C** COOKED RED KIDNEY BEANS

I **C** CORN KERNELS

¹/₂ **t** LEMON JUICE

I **T** GRATED CHEDDAR CHEESE

Mock Duck Noodle Soup

Serves 6

Briefly sauté herbs and spices together in the oil in a saucepan. Add water and gluten and bring to a boil. Add soy sauce, celery and noodles, cover, and simmer 5 minutes. Add remaining ingredients. Reheat, season and serve.

RICE:

2 **C** RAW BASMATI OR SUSHI RICE,
COOKED IN 4 **C** WATER

$^1/_2$ **t** SALT

$^1/_2$ **T** SUGAR

I **T** VINEGAR

FILLING:

$^1/_4$ **lb** TOFU ($^1/_4$ PACKAGE),
MARINATED

2 **C** SHREDDED FRESH SPINACH LEAF,
STEAMED LIGHTLY

I JALAPENO PEPPER, FINELY CHOPPED

MARINADE FOR TOFU:

I **t** FRESHLY GRATED FRESH GINGER
ROOT

2 **T** SOY SAUCE

OTHER INGREDIENTS:

4 SHEETS SUSHI NORI,
8 INCHES SQUARE

Sushi

Makes four 8-inch sushi rolls

Cook the rice with salt, sugar, and vinegar. Meanwhile, marinate the tofu in the soy sauce and ginger. When the rice is cooked, place a sheet of nori on a slightly larger piece of foil. Cover with a half inch layer of rice, leaving a margin of $^3/_4$ inches along opposite sides of the seaweed. Place a line of filling parallel to the margins, down the center of the rice. Roll up the seaweed to make a spiral roll, using the foil to support and guide the rolling; and using the outer margin to seal the sushi. Wrap tightly in foil and leave to cool, then slice into rounds and serve with wasabi mustard, a hot Japanese mustard made with horseradish, available from Asian stores.

I **C** FINELY CHOPPED CARROTS
I **C** FINELY CHOPPED CELERY
I **C** FINELY CHOPPED BELL PEPPER
2 **t** GROUND CORIANDER SEED
2 **t** GRATED FRESH GINGER ROOT
2 TO 3 BAY LEAVES
I **t** PAPRIKA
$^1/_2$ **t** WHOLE NIGELLA SEED
$^1/_2$ **t** FENUGREEK SEED
$^1/_4$ **t** TURMERIC
$^1/_4$ **t** WHOLE CARDAMOM SEED
  (REMOVE FROM POD)
2 **t** GROUND CUMIN
I **T** OIL (FOR SAUTÉING)
I **C** CHOPPED PINEAPPLE CHUNKS
5 **T** TOMATO PASTE
2 **T** BROWN SUGAR
3 **T** CIDER VINEGAR
I **T** SOY SAUCE
I SMALL CAN BABY CORN SPEARS
I **T** CAPERS
4 **C** WATER
SALT AND PEPPER
2 **T** CORNSTARCH, DISSOLVED IN A
  LITTLE COLD WATER

24-ingredient Sweet and Sour Sauce
Serves 4-6

Briefly sauté the fresh vegetables and spices in oil in a large saucepan and cover with water. Simmer until vegetables are tender. Add all the other ingredients except cornstarch. Then add cornstarch, stirring constantly. Continue to stir until the sauce thickens. Serve with rice, tofu dishes, steamed vegetables, and/or noodles.

Recipes from Mexico

3 T OIL

10 CORN TORTILLAS

1 1/2 C GRATED PARMESAN CHEESE

<u>FILLING:</u>

1 BATCH BLACKEYED PEAS
   IN HERB SAUCE (P. 23)

1 C BREAD CRUMBS

1/2 PACK (5 OZ) FROZEN SPINACH,
   THAWED

<u>SAUCE:</u>

2 LARGE OR 4 SMALL TOMATOES,
   FINELY CHOPPED

2 MEDIUM BELL PEPPERS, FINELY
   CHOPPED

1 t ASAFETIDA (HING) (P. 196)

1 t CHILI POWDER

2 T BUTTER (FOR SAUTÉING)

2 T TAHINI

3/4 C WATER

2 T SOY SAUCE

SALT AND FRESHLY GROUND
   BLACK PEPPER TO TASTE

Enchiladas
Serves 5

Make the Blackeyed Peas in Herb
Sauce with 2 C cooked beans and
2 C milk, as in the recipe. Add the
bread crumbs and spinach. Set
aside. In a heavy skillet, warm 3 T
oil and dip each tortilla into it
briefly. The oil will soften the
tortillas and make them flexible.
Alternatively, place the tortillas in a
plastic bag and heat briefly (1 minute) in a microwave oven. Set
aside.

Now make the sauce: In a
separate skillet or frying pan sauté
the tomatoes and bell pepper in the
butter with the chili powder and
asafetida for 5 minutes. Dissolve
the tahini in half the water, stirring
vigorously until smooth. Add the
tahini mixture to the vegetables
and mix. Add the soy sauce and
the rest of the water to the pan and
cook for 3 to 5 minutes more. In
an oiled 10-inch x 12-inch
casserole dish, roll up a little of the
filling in each tortilla. Arrange the
tortillas in the casserole dish,
leaving a space down the middle,
and pour the sauce into this. Cover
all with grated parmesan cheese
and bake for 10 minutes at 375°.
Serve with a green salad.

FLESH OF 2 MEDIUM AVOCADOS

I LARGE TOMATO, PEELED

I t PAPRIKA

PINCH OF CAYENNE

SALT AND PEPPER

3 T LEMON JUICE

I T OLIVE OIL

¹/₈ t MACE

SPRIG OF PARSLEY OR CILANTRO FOR

   GARNISH

Guacamole

Serves 4

Blend. Adjust seasoning, adding more of anything at all until you like the taste. Keep well-covered before serving, or the surface will discolor.

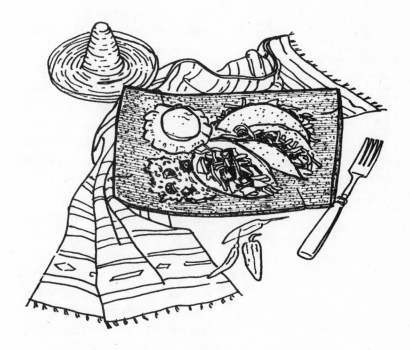

Recipes from Europe

9 MEDIUM-SIZED POTATOES

4 T OIL FOR POTATOES

I t ROSEMARY

SALT AND FRESHLY MILLED BLACK
  PEPPER TO TASTE

I LARGE EGGPLANT, SLICED

5 T OIL FOR EGGPLANT

I t PAPRIKA

I t GROUND CORIANDER SEED

I t OREGANO

I MEDIUM WHITE CABBAGE (**4 ½**
  INCHES DIAMETER)

6 C MILK

³/₄ t NUTMEG

³/₄ t MACE

2 OZ (**½** STICK) BUTTER

2 BAY LEAVES

4½ T CORNSTARCH, DISSOLVED
  IN A LITTLE COLD WATER

I ⅓ C GRATED CHEDDAR CHEESE

2 TO 3 LARGE TOMATOES, PEELED
  AND SLICED

Moussaka

Serves 6

This is not at all like the classical Greek dish really, but I had fun putting this truly "alternative" vegetarian version together.

Boil the potatoes until barely tender. Allow to cool, and peel the skins. In a large heavy skillet heat 4 T oil and sauté the potatoes with rosemary until they are crisp and golden on the surface. Transfer contents of skillet to a large oiled casserole dish. Sprinkle salt and pepper over potatoes. Wipe out the skillet and reheat remaining oil. Sauté eggplant until translucent, with paprika, coriander and oregano. Add the cabbage, very finely chopped, plus a little water just to prevent the cabbage burning. Stir fry and steam for 5 minutes until cabbage is tender. Pour the eggplant and cabbage in a layer over the potatoes. In a large stock pan heat the milk with nutmeg, mace, butter, and bay leaves until almost boiling and add the cornstarch to thicken, stirring constantly. When thick, remove from heat and add cheese. Stir until cheese melts. Pour this mixture over the potatoes, cabbage and eggplant, and decorate with slices of tomato. Bake the casserole uncovered at 300° for 15 to 20 minutes until bubbling hot. Serve with salad and chutney.

SAUCE:
(COVERS ONE 12-INCH PIZZA
  BASE)

SAUCE:

1 LARGE TOMATO

1 T OIL (FOR SAUTÉING)

¹/₂ t MARJORAM

1 t DRY BASIL LEAF

1 ¹/₂ C WATER

2 SMALL CANS TOMATO PASTE

1 T CORNSTARCH, DISSOLVED IN A
  LITTLE WATER

SALT AND PEPPER TO TASTE

Pizza

Most store-bought pizzas contain garlic in the sauce, but it is fun and very easy to make homemade pizza, especially if you buy the dough base ready-made. Here is a recipe for pizza sauce that you can cover with a huge variety of toppings. If you prefer to make the dough from scratch, the bread recipe (p. 146) can be used. Make the entire batch and freeze in small batches to use for individual pizzas. A large ball the size of your fist is about right for a 12-inch pizza base.

Briefly sauté tomato in oil in a heavy skillet with herbs and add water and tomato paste. Simmer gently for 5 minutes. Add cornstarch, stirring constantly. Season to taste with salt and pepper. Spread over pizza bases.

Toppings:
These go on next. Try sweet corn, spinach, fresh tomato, thinly sliced zucchini, fresh herbs, olives, capers, pineapple, green and red bell peppers, chili pepper flakes, tofu pieces (smoke flavor is good), cold cooked beans, etc., in any combinations you like, finishing off with a thick layer of grated cheddar or mozzarella cheese and a generous scattering of oregano.

Bake at 425° for about 6 to 7 minutes, or until cheese is well-melted and dough base is done.

Pizza á la Genovesia

This is a favorite Italian pizza which is made without any sauce. Make a bread dough with whole wheat flour (p. 146). Roll it out thinly on an oiled tray. Cover it with a sprinkling of olive oil, sea salt, and rosemary. Poke holes at regular intervals in the dough like this (this is important). Bake 10 minutes at 425° until crispy.

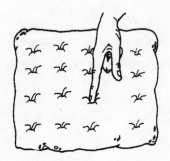

3 T OIL
I C CHOPPED GREEN OR RED
· PEPPERS
I C SLICED ZUCCHINI
I C DICED EGGPLANT
I C TOMATOES, QUARTERED
I t OREGANO
I t DRIED BASIL
SALT AND BLACK PEPPER TO TASTE

Ratatouille
Serves 4

Heat oil in a large heavy saucepan and stir-fry all the vegetables with the herbs for 10 minutes. Turn down heat and let them simmer in their own juice, but stir regularly. Cook for half an hour, adding a little water if necessary, to prevent burning. Season well with salt and black pepper.

3 ¹/₂ **C** RAW BROWN RICE

3 STALKS CELERY

¹/₄ TO ¹/₂ **C** OIL (FOR SAUTÉING)

3 LARGE FRESH BUNCHES DILL

1 LARGE BUNCH PARSLEY

SALT

JUICE OF 3 LEMONS

2 LARGE JARS GRAPE LEAVES —
  ABOUT 150 OF THEM

Stuffed Vine Leaves

Nice for Thanksgiving feasts
Makes about 150 (can be
frozen)

Salted vine leaves can be
bought ready-cooked from
Greek delicatessens.
Traditionally they are stuffed
with rice to which a little
flavoring has been added. A
little of the filling is placed on
each leaf, then the leaf is rolled
into a small parcel and baked
in the oven until hot. This
recipe feeds 30 people, and can
be halved or quartered for
smaller amounts.

Cook the rice (p. 10). Chop
celery very finely and sauté in
oil until clear. Sort out the
tough stems from the dill and
parsley, and chop the rest fine.
Add to celery and sauté briefly.
Add the rice, salt and lemon
juice, mix well and sauté a
little longer. Rinse the grape
leaves well and boil in water
for 15 minutes. Put a little of
the rice mixture at the base of
each grape leaf, fold in the
sides, and roll up. Place them
snugly on an oiled baking pan,
using a pastry brush to brush
the tops with a little olive oil.
Bake at 350° for about 20
minutes.

SAUCE:

1 LARGE GREEN PEPPER
8 TOMATOES, SKINNED
2 TO 3 BAY LEAVES
2 TO 3 T FRESH PARSLEY, FINELY
 CHOPPED
2 t BASIL
2 t OREGANO
1 T OLIVE OIL (FOR SAUTÉING)
4 T TOMATO PASTE
SALT AND PEPPER TO TASTE

OTHER INGREDIENTS:

12 SHEETS LASAGNA PASTA
1 TUB (15 OZ) RICOTTA CHEESE
2 C GRATED MOZZARELLA CHEESE
6 C SHREDDED FRESH SPINACH
 (7 1/2 OZ)

Note: This lasagna has a very delicate flavor. For a stronger flavor substitute mature cheddar for the Italian cheeses. You will need almost 5 C, grated. TVP can also be added to the tomato sauce, in which case it will need a little extra water or vegetable stock and tomato paste added too.

Spinach-Ricotta Lasagna
Serves 6-8

Chop peppers finely. Chop tomatoes. Sauté herbs and vegetables in the oil very briefly, add the tomato paste, then let all sauce ingredients cook slowly for 15 to 20 minutes. Use your heaviest pot and stir often. If the sauce is too thick to flow, add a little water. While the sauce is cooking, boil the pasta in salted water until it is soft but not soggy — about 10 minutes. Now oil a deep rectangular casserole dish and make your lasagna as follows:

- A layer of pasta, laid flat (just overlapping)
- A layer of ricotta cheese
- Cover with sauce
- A layer of raw spinach
- A layer of pasta
- A layer of ricotta cheese
- Cover with sauce
- Another layer of spinach

Repeat until you have no more room, finishing with a layer of mozzarella cheese. I use an 11-inch x 13-inch dish with 4 strips to each layer (3 layers). Bake the lasagna at 350° for about 30 to 35 minutes, covering with aluminum foil. Remove the foil for the last 10 minutes so the cheese browns. Serve with a crisp green salad.

$^1/_2$ **C** GRATED PARMESAN CHEESE

PINCH OF ALLSPICE OR NUTMEG,
FRESHLY GROUND

SALT

$^1/_4$ **C** OLIVE OIL

2 C LOOSELY PACKED FRESH SWEET
BASIL LEAVES

$^1/_2$ **C** GROUND PINE NUTS OR
WALNUTS

Yvonne's Pesto
Serves 4

Absolutely delicious.

In a blender combine cheese,
spices, salt, oil and basil. Add
nuts gradually, for as long as
your blender can take them.
Add the rest in afterward,
crushed. Serve on pasta.

Recipes from Africa

**3 LARGE PLANTAINS (SKINS ARE
   BLACK WHEN RIPE)**
**I TO I ¹/₂ C PEANUT OIL
   (SHOULD BE AT LEAST I-INCH
   DEEP IN PAN)**
I ¹/₂ t GINGER POWDER
¹/₂ t CHILI POWDER
SALT TO TASTE

Fried Plantain
Serves 6

Slice the plantains thinly. Heat
oil in a heavy saucepan, until a
small piece of bread sinks, rises
sizzling, and browns in 10 to
15 seconds. Fry the plantain
slices a few at a time until
crisp, removing with a slotted
spoon, and drain. Toss in a
brown paper bag with salt and
spices, and serve warm.

I lb FRESH OKRA
¹/₂ C WATER
I t SALT
2 MEDIUM TOMATOES, CHOPPED
¹/₂ t CHILI POWDER

Sauce Gombo
Serves 3-4

Top, tail, and slice the okra in
rounds. Place all ingredients in
a saucepan and simmer until
tender. Serve with Yam Fou
Fou (next).

6 LARGE YAMS
3 T RICE FLOUR
1 T WARM WATER
SALT AND FRESHLY MILLED BLACK
   PEPPER TO TASTE

Yam Fou Fou
Serves 6

Peel yams, cut into large pieces and boil until tender, then drain and mash them. Stir in the rice flour, salt, and pepper with the water and continue mashing until smooth. Re-heat gently and serve.

3 C DARK GREENS, SHREDDED
1 T PEANUT OIL (FOR SAUTÉING)
3 C WATER
1 T FLOUR, DISSOLVED IN A LITTLE
   COLD WATER
2 C COOKED LIMA BEANS OR
   OTHER WHITE BEANS
2 T FINELY CRUSHED OR GROUND
   ROASTED PEANUTS
SALT AND FRESHLY MILLED BLACK
   PEPPER TO TASTE

Ugali
Serves 3-4

In a heavy saucepan, sauté greens in oil briefly and cover with water. Bring to a boil and simmer until tender. Gradually add the flour, stirring constantly until the mixture thickens. Add the other ingredients and simmer, stirring constantly for 5 minutes.

3 LARGE GREEN PLANTAINS
4 T LEMON JUICE
2 T PEANUT OIL (FOR SAUTÉING)
1 LARGE TOMATO, PEELED AND
   CHOPPED FINE
SALT AND FRESHLY GROUND BLACK
   PEPPER TO TASTE

Plantain Casserole
Serves 6

Peel and slice the plantains 1 inch thick. Dip in lemon juice and sauté them in oil over low heat, stirring constantly. Add tomato and seasoning and transfer to an oiled casserole dish with a lid. Bake at 275° for 1 ½ hours.

Chapter 9

Salads

Salads are fun to make, and with a little imagination they can be made in infinite varieties. Most cooked meals are brightened up with some salad, however simple it may be. Salads are also necessary for our health and it is important to make sure that you eat raw vegetables every day. If you have never experimented very much with salads, here are some vegetables that can be used:

lettuce

tomatoes

cucumber

celery and celery root

grated carrots and carrot leaves

cubed cooked carrots

cooked peas

cooked sweet corn

beets (raw and cooked) and their leaves

watercress

apples, oranges, grapes, pineapple, coconut, melon

nuts

seaweed

cold steamed okra

cauliflower and broccoli

red and green peppers

fennel bulbs

cabbage; red, white, Chinese

cooked potatoes

spinach

turnip leaves

fresh dill

fresh mint

fresh parsley

cilantro

endive

avocados

seed, grain, and bean sprouts

capers

olives

cheese cubes (any variety)
cold cooked rice
cold cooked wheatberries
roasted sunflower seeds
cold cooked bulgur wheat
cold pasta
tofu
cold cooked beans and peas
garden rocket (an herb with leaves similar to dandelion leaves)
chard
nasturtium flowers or young scented geranium petals

I BUNCH FRESH CELERY
5 OR 6 TART APPLES
I T LEMON JUICE
3 T SOUR CREAM
I T APPLE CIDER VINEGAR
I T FRESH CHOPPED MINT OR I t
  DRIED MINT
¹/₂ C CHOPPED WALNUTS
I T RAISINS
SALT AND PEPPER

Celery, Apple, and Walnut Salad
Serves 4-6

Chop the celery and apples quite small. When the apples are chopped, squeeze lemon juice on them to prevent them going brown. Mix the cream, vinegar, and mint together and add to the salad with the walnuts and raisins. Season with salt and pepper to taste.

2 C COLD COOKED BULGUR WHEAT
   (P. 17)
1 C FINELY CHOPPED FRESH PARSLEY
½ C CHOPPED TOMATOES

DRESSING:
JUICE OF 1 LEMON
2 T TAHINI
SALT AND PEPPER
½ t PAPRIKA

Tabbouleh Salad

Serves 2-3

Blend tahini and lemon juice
until smooth. Add other
ingredients.

3 lb NEW POTATOES
1 LARGE CUCUMBER
½ C FRESH OR FROZEN PEAS OR
   SWEET CORN
2 C SHREDDED SPINACH LEAF
1 HEAD ICEBERG LETTUCE

DRESSING:
1 C PLAIN YOGURT
1 C COTTAGE CHEESE
3 T OLIVE OIL
3 T CIDER VINEGAR
2 T EACH FINELY CHOPPED FRESH
   MINT AND PARSLEY
SALT AND BLACK PEPPER TO TASTE

Potato Salad
Serves 8-10

A good filling meal for a hot
day; great for a picnic.

Boil the potatoes without peeling
them. Meanwhile, chop the
cucumber, tomatoes and
peppers. Cook the peas and/or
corn.
   Blend all the ingredients of
the dressing together. When the
potatoes are cooked, pour on the
dressing while still hot, and then
allow to cool. Mix gently with all
the other ingredients except
lettuce. Arrange the lettuce
leaves around the side of a salad
bowl and place the potato salad
in the middle. Decorate with
cress. To make this salad more of
a complete meal, cold lima beans
can be added. Prepare the beans
from the recipe on page 22.

1 ¹/₂ LARGE CUCUMBERS

SOME SPRIGS OF PARSLEY, CHOPPED
VERY FINELY

1 C PLAIN YOGURT

1 T LEMON JUICE

1 T FRESH DILL LEAF, FINELY MINCED

SALT

Cucumber Salad

Serves 4-6

Grate the cucumbers and sprinkle with salt — this will draw out some of the water. Leave to drain for an hour in a cool place. Then mix all ingredients well and serve.

1 BUNCH WATERCRESS, CHOPPED

DRESSING:

4 t OLIVE OIL

JUICE OF HALF A LIME

¹/₂ t GRATED FRESH GINGER ROOT

1 t WHOLE GRAIN MUSTARD

SALT AND BLACK PEPPER TO TASTE

Watercress and Ginger Salad

Serves 2-3

Combine all ingredients.

- 1 SMALL HEAD ICEBERG LETTUCE
- 1 ½ C GRATED APPLE, SPRINKLED WITH LEMON
- 1 C GRAPES WITH PITS REMOVED, OR PINEAPPLE CUBES
- 8 OZ CREAM CHEESE, SOFTENED
- 4 TOMATOES
- 1 BUNCH WATERCRESS

Cream Cheese Salad
Serves 3-4

Arrange the lettuce leaves in a dish, and the apple near the edge of the lettuce. Mix the grapes or pineapple with the cream cheese and place it in the center of the dish. Decorate the salad with tomatoes and watercress.

- 2 C SWEET CORN KERNELS
- 2 C COTTAGE CHEESE
- 1 GREEN PEPPER, SEEDED AND CHOPPED FINE
- PINCH OF PAPRIKA
- PINCH OF CAYENNE PEPPER
- 1 t WHOLE GRAIN MUSTARD

Sweet Corn and Cottage Cheese Salad
Serves 3-4

Cook and cool the corn and mix it with the cheese and the pepper. Add paprika, cayenne pepper, and mustard.

2 **C** GRATED CARROTS

I **C** SOUR CREAM

I **C** CHOPPED CILANTRO (OPTIONAL)

Creamy Carrot Salad

Serves 3-4

Mix together and serve.

I **C** DRY ARAME (SEAWEED)

I SMALL CAULIFLOWER, BROKEN INTO
    FLORETS

2 **C** BROCCOLI FLORETS

I BELL PEPPER, FINELY CHOPPED

I **C** BEAN SPROUTS

I **C** GREEN BEANS, COOKED AND
    COOLED

I **T** SUNFLOWER OIL

2 **T** LEMON JUICE

I **t** GRATED FRESH GINGER ROOT

$^1/_2$ **t** PAPRIKA

I **T** SOY SAUCE

3 **T** TOASTED SUNFLOWER SEEDS

SALT AND FRESHLY MILLED BLACK
    PEPPER TO TASTE

Arame Broccoli Salad

Serves 4-6

Soak and boil arame according
to the instructions on the
package. Drain and allow to
cool. Meanwhile, steam the
cauliflower and broccoli until
barely tender. When arame and
vegetables cool, combine all
ingredients and serve.

8 OZ TOFU
¹/₂ LARGE OR I SMALL AVOCADO
2 C COOKED PASTA SPIRALS
²/₃ C SOUR CREAM
¹/₂ t PAPRIKA
¹/₄ t NUTMEG
¹/₂ t GROUND CORIANDER SEED
¹/₂ T CAPERS, PLUS I t OF THE BRINE
¹/₈ t MACE
¹/₄ t GINGER POWDER
I t LEMON JUICE
SALT AND FRESHLY GROUND BLACK
   PEPPER TO TASTE

Tofu Pasta Avocado Salad
Serves 3-4

Cut the tofu and avocado into small pieces. Combine all ingredients.

2 C SNOW PEAS (MANGETOUTS)
I CAN WATER CHESTNUTS, DRAINED
   AND SLICED
2 C SHREDDED CHINESE CABBAGE

DRESSING:
¹/₂ t FRESHLY GRATED GINGER ROOT
3 T SUNFLOWER OIL
2 T ROSEMARY HERBED VINEGAR
PINCH OF SALT

Snow Pea Salad
Serves 4

Mix.
Serve dressing separately.

2 LARGE FIRM TOMATOES
1 SMALL GREEN PEPPER, SEEDED
$^1/_2$ CUCUMBER
$^1/_2$ C SPROUTED GREEN LENTILS
A FEW LEAVES WATERCRESS
2 T SUNFLOWER SEEDS
2 C COOKED WHOLE WHEATBERRIES
   (P. 16)

DRESSING:
JUICE OF 1 LEMON
$^1/_2$ t GRATED FRESH GINGER ROOT
2 T SUNFLOWER OIL
SALT AND PEPPER TO TASTE

Wheat Salad
Serves 4

Chop up all vegetables and mix them into the wheatberries. Sprinkle with the dressing and serve.

4 HEADS ENDIVE, CUT LENGTHWISE IN
   QUARTERS
2 LARGE ORANGES, PEELED AND CUT

DRESSING:
4 T PLAIN YOGURT
1 T HONEY
GRATED RIND OF $^1/_4$ TO $^1/_2$ ORANGE
   (TO TASTE) AND A LITTLE JUICE
   (NOTE: USE ONLY THE COLORED
   PART OF THE RIND)
3 T OIL
1 T VINEGAR
SALT AND PEPPER TO TASTE

Endive and Orange Salad
Serves 4-6

For this, only white-leaved endive should be used. The green-edged leaves are bitter.

Combine all ingredients and serve.

Endive and Apple Salad

Use apples instead of oranges
in the Endive Salad recipe, and
use lemon juice in the dressing
instead of orange peel and
juice.

2 T FINELY CHOPPED FRESH PARSLEY

2 C COOKED CHICKPEAS

¹/₂ C CHOPPED, SKINNED TOMATOES

¹/₂ C CHOPPED BELL PEPPER

1 ¹/₂ C SHREDDED SPINACH LEAVES

DRESSING:

1 ¹/₂ T OLIVE OIL

1 T WINE VINEGAR

1 t OREGANO

SALT AND FRESHLY GROUND BLACK
   PEPPER TO TASTE

¹/₂ t DRY BASIL LEAF

Chickpea Salad
Serves 3-4

Combine all ingredients and
serve.

2 T FINELY CHOPPED FRESH PARSLEY

2 C COOKED RED KIDNEY BEANS

1/2 C CHOPPED SKINNED TOMATOES

1/2 C CHOPPED BELL PEPPER

1/2 C FENUGREEK SPROUTS

DRESSING:

2 T OLIVE OIL

2 T TARRAGON HERBED VINEGAR

SALT AND FRESHLY MILLED BLACK
  PEPPER TO TASTE

Red Bean Salad

Serves 3-4

Combine all ingredients and serve.

2 VERY FRESH SMALL TO MEDIUM
  BEETS WITH LEAVES

1 C FRESH PARSLEY, CHOPPED

DRESSING:

USE THE CAPER DIP RECIPE (P. 140)
  BUT HALVE THE QUANTITIES.

Raw Beet Salad

Serves 3-4

Cut the leaves and stem from the beets (save the freshest green leaves). Scrub the beets but do not peel them. Grate the flesh and combine it with the shredded green leaves and parsley. Stir the caper dip into the salad.

I HEAD LETTUCE

¹/₂ C FETA CHEESE, CUT IN CUBES

¹/₂ C OLIVES, PITTED

¹/₂ C TOMATOES, SKINNED AND
    QUARTERED

¹/₂ CUCUMBER, CUBED

I t POPPY SEED (FOR GARNISH)

DRESSING:

¹/₂ C PLAIN YOGURT

I T OLIVE OIL

I T LEMON JUICE

SALT AND BLACK PEPPER TO TASTE

Greek Salad
Serves 4-6

Arrange lettuce around the edges of a bowl. Combine cheese, olives, tomatoes, and cucumber. Mix with dressing. Place this in the center. Garnish with poppy seed.

Dressings

4 T OLIVE OIL (NUT OIL CAN BE USED)

3 T LEMON JUICE OR CIDER VINEGAR

SALT AND PEPPER TO TASTE

French Dressing
Serves 4

Blend oil, lemon (or vinegar), and seasoning. This dressing is usually used for green salads of lettuce, tomatoes, cucumber, and peas.

4 T SUNFLOWER OIL
2 T LEMON JUICE
I T CLEAR HONEY
I ¹/₂ T FRESH OR I t DRIED MINT
(OPTIONAL)

4 T SUNFLOWER OIL
4 T CIDER VINEGAR
SALT AND PEPPER TO TASTE
I T FRESH HERBS (MINT OR PARSLEY)
OR DRIED HERBS (BASIL OR THYME)

2 T TAHINI
JUICE OF 2 LEMONS
2 T YOGURT
SALT TO TASTE

Lemon, Oil and Honey Dressing
Serves 4

You can blend these in a blender or food processor, or heat the honey gently until it is thin enough to blend in with the other ingredients. This dressing is good for salads containing sweet vegetables (for example, carrots, beets, fennel).

Cider Vinegar Dressing
Serves 4

Mix ingredients. This is a good all-purpose salad dressing, and you can experiment with different herbs.

Tahini and Lemon Dressing
Serves 4

Tahini is a butter made from finely crushed roasted sesame seeds. It is available from Middle Eastern delicatessens or whole food stores. It makes a fine dressing for salads and a spread for bread, and can be used as a thickener in soups and stews. Tahini has a rich, nutty flavor and is rich in calcium.

Blend the tahini and lemon with salt, and when thoroughly blended, add the yogurt. Good for heavy salads such as those made with rice, bulgur, or beans.

¹/₂ **C** PLAIN YOGURT
¹/₂ **C** COTTAGE CHEESE
2 T SUNFLOWER OIL
2 T LEMON JUICE
¹/₂ **t** CARAWAY SEEDS OR SOME FRESH
   CHOPPED HERBS

Yogurt and Cheese Dressing

For cabbage salads.
Serves 4

Blend.

¹/₂ **C** PLAIN YOGURT
2 T CIDER VINEGAR
JUICE OF **I** LEMON
SALT, PEPPER,
I t DRIED MINT OR **2 t** FRESH

Sour Dressing

Serves 4

Blend. Good with avocado.

I C NORWEGIAN BROWN CHEESE,
   GRATED
2 T HONEY
2 T APPLE CIDER VINEGAR
PINCH OF MACE
PINCH OF SALT

Brown Cheese Dressing

Serves 4

Blend. This is a very sweet dressing, good with strongly flavored raw greens like spinach and beet leaves. Try also on grated raw beet.

Chapter 10

Party and Buffet Food

Use the following recipes for little snacks which look attractive and are fairly easy to eat with a fork or fingers. If you are making a buffet table it is important to include as large a variety of different textures and flavors as possible. For instance: one type of sandwich, one pastry dish, one or two salads, a cheese dip, some little savory biscuits, crackers, scones and fresh fruit, nuts and raisins would be a good variety of different foods. Also try Sushi (p. 110) and Dim Sum (p. 108) as buffet food. Bread sticks (p. 151) are delicious to serve at a party as an alternative to biscuits, rolls, etc.

Dips and Patés

To be served with slices of whole wheat bread cut into fingers, chips, or raw vegetables.

Hummus

The recipe for Hummus (p. 24) is a good party dip and filling for sandwiches.

2 C COOKED BLACKEYED PEAS
(P. 23), PLUS A LITTLE OF THE
COOKING WATER
I C COTTAGE CHEESE
3 T TAHINI
¹/₂ t MARJORAM
³/₄ t SAGE
³/₄ t PAPRIKA
PINCH CHILI POWDER
³/₄ t GROUND CORIANDER SEED
4 TO 5 T FRESH CHOPPED PARSLEY
I T LEMON JUICE
I T CAPER BRINE
¹/₈ t THYME
¹/₄ t NUTMEG
¹/₈ t TURMERIC
SALT AND PEPPER TO TASTE

Cottage Cheese and Blackeyed Pea Paté
Serves 4-6

Have fun combining all these wonderful flavorings. Multiple herbs and spices are fast to combine once you develop a feel of how much to use. Always go easy on the turmeric.

Blend to a smooth texture.

I LARGE EGGPLANT
¹/₂ C WALNUTS
2 T OLIVE OIL
SALT AND PEPPER TO TASTE
I t PAPRIKA
PINCH OF CAYENNE PEPPER, OR A
DASH OF HOT PEPPER SAUCE
PARSLEY OR WATERCRESS TO
GARNISH

Eggplant Walnut Dip
Serves 4-6

Prick eggplant, wrap in foil. Bake whole for about 40 minutes at 350° until tender. Put walnuts in the oven and bake for 5 minutes with eggplant, then chop finely or grind. When the eggplant is done, cut in half and scoop out the flesh. Place the flesh in a blender with oil, salt, pepper, paprika, and cayenne and combine. When smooth, turn into a bowl, mix with walnuts, garnish and serve.

½ **C** SOUR CREAM
¼ **C** SOY MAYONNAISE
½ **T** MUSTARD, PREPARED IN
  ADVANCE WITH WATER
4 T FINELY CHOPPED FRESH DILL
SALT AND PEPPER TO TASTE

Sour Cream and Dill Dip

Blend.

4 T SOY MAYONNAISE
4 T SOUR CREAM
2 T THYME-TARRAGON HERBED
  VINEGAR
I t CAPERS
SALT AND FRESHLY GROUND BLACK
  PEPPER TO TASTE

Caper Dip
Serves 3-4

Mix.

1 BUNCH WATERCRESS
2 T LEMON JUICE
1 T HERBED VINEGAR
¹/₂ C SOY MAYONNAISE
HALF A LARGE TOMATO, CHOPPED
4 T COARSELY CHOPPED CILANTRO
SALT AND FRESHLY MILLED BLACK
   PEPPER TO TASTE

Chunky Watercress Dip
Serves 3-4

Very tangy.

Blend ²/₃ of the watercress in a blender with lemon, vinegar, and mayonnaise until smooth. Coarsely chop the remaining watercress and stir into the blended ingredients, together with the tomato and cilantro. Add salt and pepper.

Stuffed Items

Also try Stuffed Peppers (p. 47), Stuffed Baked Potatoes (p. 52), Vine Leaves (p. 117) or Zucchini Canoes (p. 59).

1 CUCUMBER

FILLING:
¹/₂ C CREAM CHEESE
¹/₂ t PAPRIKA
A LITTLE WATERCRESS, WALNUTS,
   SWEET CORN, OR WHATEVER YOU
   LIKE

Stuffed Cucumber
Serves 3-4

Slice the cucumber into 1-inch rounds. With a sharp knife, cut out most of the center. Set this aside. Fill the centers with the cream cheese mixture and arrange in a bowl.

2 APPLES

1 STICK CELERY

PINCH SALT

LEMON JUICE

6 LARGE, FIRM TOMATOES

1 OR 2 T FRENCH DRESSING

1 OR 2 T THICK CREAM (FRESH OR
SOUR)

PINCH TARRAGON

2 OZ CHOPPED WALNUTS

Cold Stuffed Tomatoes
Serves 6

Chop apple and celery and
sprinkle with a pinch of salt
and some lemon juice. Cut the
tops off the tomatoes and
scoop out the seeds and juice.
Mix together French dressing
and cream, and pour them over
the apple and celery. Add
walnuts and tarragon, mix, and
fill the tomatoes.

Stuffed Celery Sticks

Fill crisp sticks of celery with
cream cheese, walnuts, and
grapes. To do this, chop
walnuts finely, mix with halved
and pitted grapes, and mash in
the cream cheese. Combine all
quantities to taste. To make the
celery extra crisp, soak
beforehand for 30 minutes in
chilled water. Arrange them on
a pretty plate. Serve with whole
grain mustard and gomasio
(next page) for dipping and
sprinkling.

Crispy Filled Rolls

Having tried various fillings for stuffing vegetables, you might like to try making stuffed croustades (crisp, filled bread rolls). For this you take several crusty rolls and cut them in half. Scoop out the crumbs, leaving the crusts hollow. Brush the crusts inside and out with melted butter and bake them at 300° for 10 to 15 minutes, until they have turned crisp. Meanwhile, prepare your filling. You can use any of the fillings listed for stuffing tomatoes, peppers, celery, etc., or any other vegetable stuffing recipe. Avoid very wet fillings such as puréed beans, as they tend to make the rolls soggy again. When the rolls and filling are ready, place some of the filling in each one and replace the top. They make a nice surprise on a buffet table.

3 ¹/₂ C UNHULLED SESAME SEEDS
¹/₂ C SALT

Gomasio
Makes 4 cups

A gift to the world's condiment cuisine from Japan.
Toast sesame seeds in a large heavy skillet until evenly browned. Beware of seeds popping. When toasted, grind to a meal in an electric grinder with salt. Put into airtight jars, and use as a condiment for sprinkling on food.

Chapter 11

Breads

Smell it baking in the oven...mmm! Cut off the crust while it's still crisp and warm and enjoy eating it. Bread is alive, and to make it is pure satisfaction. If you feel daunted by what appears to be a complicated scientific process, try making unleavened bread.

Take some whole wheat flour (any quantity), add a pinch of salt. Mix in water until it holds together. Bend, twist, roll, squeeze, and punch it for a few minutes, then form it into a round and put it on a baking tray. Bake at 425° until it is brown. This is bread of the simplest kind.

Other kinds of breads are yeast, sourdough bread, soda bread, with rye flour, maize, oats, barley — with or without fat, sometimes with milk, malt, fruit, or spices in it. Following is a recipe for ordinary yeasted whole wheat bread. Try to obtain organically grown, stone-ground flour of local origin to ensure freshness, nutrients, and flavor.

2 T THICK, DARK MOLASSES, AND 2 OZ CRUMBLED FRESH YEAST (OR 1 OZ DRY YEAST), MIXED WITH 1 C LUKEWARM WATER

3 lb WHOLE WHEAT FLOUR (10 ½ C)

2 OZ (½ STICK) BUTTER OR ⅔ C OIL

1 T SALT

Whole Wheat Bread
Makes 3 large loaves

Before you begin, warm the kitchen and heat the oven to 425°. Place the yeast mixture in a warm place where it can liven up and leave it 15 minutes until it is frothy. (The yeast eats the sugar and produces carbon dioxide as a waste gas, which is what makes the bread rise.) Warm a large mixing bowl and the flour by putting them in the oven for just a minute. When the yeast is frothy, it is ready. Rub the butter and salt into the flour for a few minutes. Make a well in the center of the flour and pour in the yeast mixture. Mix it in and continue adding warm water a little at a time until the dough is moist, but not wet. When it is holding together, transfer it to a floured board and begin to knead it vigorously. Go on, punch it! Twist it

around, fold it over and punch it in all directions until it is smooth, spongy, and elastic — like a cushion. After a while, it will stop sticking to your hands; it helps to dip them in warm water from time to time. The dough, when ready, should not squelch; if it does it's too wet, so add some extra flour by kneading the bread into flour sprinkled on the board. If it becomes very stiff and dry you can add a little more water. The longer you knead it, the nicer it will be: about 15 minutes is sufficient. A food processor with a dough hook will also perform this strenuous task. Now divide the dough into 3 large or 4 smaller lumps and make them into loaf shapes. Put them into warmed oiled bread pans and leave them in a gently warm place, undisturbed by movement or fluctuations in temperature, to rise. Meanwhile, preheat the oven to 425°. Check them after 20 minutes. They should rise until nearly twice the original size, and the time it will take seems to vary. When they've risen enough, transfer them to the oven. After 10 minutes, turn it down to 375°, and bake for another 25 to 30 minutes. As soon as the bread looks done, turn it out onto a wire rack. To make sure the center is cooked, you can tap the base of the loaf and listen to the sound it makes. If it sounds hollow, the bread is done, but if it sounds solid (dull thud), the bread will need a bit longer in the oven. You can cut it after half an hour, but it's better to leave it an hour or two to cool.

7 C GRANARY FLOUR*

1 ¹/₂ OZ FRESH YEAST, CRUMBLED

1 ¹/₂ T THICK, DARK MOLASSES

³/₄ T SALT

¹/₂ PINT WARM WATER

1 T OIL OR BUTTER

Granary Bread

Makes 2 large or 3 small circular loaves

*Granary flour is whole wheat flour with malted wheat grains added. It has a very distinctive flavor. If you cannot find granary flour, try regular whole wheat bread flour and substitute malt syrup for the molasses.

Warm the yeast with the molasses and salt in the lukewarm water. When it is frothy, rub the butter into the flour and knead in the yeast. After 15 minutes of kneading, form the dough into loaves (granary loaves are traditionally round) and put them in a warm place to rise. Bake 10 minutes at 410° and 25 to 30 minutes at 375°.

2 OZ YEAST DISSOLVED WITH 2 T
MOLASSES IN A LITTLE WARM MILK
7 C WHOLE WHEAT FLOUR
ABOUT 2 C WARM MILK
2 T OIL OR BUTTER
3 ¹/₂ C RYE FLOUR
I T SALT
I TO 2 t CARAWAY SEEDS, TO TASTE

Rye Bread
Makes 2 large loaves

Rye flour makes a dough heavy and sticky.

Set the yeast in a warm place to wake up. Warm the bowl, flour and milk. Rub the oil into the flour and add salt and caraway seeds. Knead in the yeast and enough milk to make a smooth dough. Knead the dough for 15 minutes, then leave it in a warm place to rise in the mixing bowl. Because rye flour is heavier than wheat flour, it usually needs to rise twice. So let your dough rise 1 hour in the mixing bowl, then punch it down again. Reknead it for 5 minutes or so and form into loaves. Set these to rise again, and when nicely formed and risen, bake them at 410° for 10 minutes, then at 325° for 20-30 minutes.

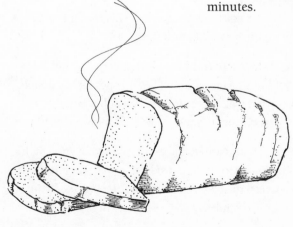

About Ingredients

YEAST

Fresh yeast makes better bread than dried yeast. It will keep in a refrigerator for 4 or 5 days, but dies if kept longer. Dead yeast is brown and caked hard (buy some more). Dried yeast is widely available and keeps longer.

MILK BREAD

Milk bread is richer, softer and sweeter than bread made with water. Simply mix warm milk into the flour instead of water. Bread baked without any oil is very crusty and crumbly, but it might crumble to pieces when you cut it. This depends on the flour.

SEEDS

To brighten the crust of your bread, press the top of the loaf into a plate of poppy or sesame seeds before you put it in the tin to rise. The seeds get toasted while the bread bakes.

Troubleshooting: If your Bread Fails

If your bread has not risen, and it's heavy and doughy:

1. Your yeast was dead or too stale to begin with.

2. You accidentally killed it by overheating it.

3. The place where you rose your bread was too hot or too cold, or the temperature kept fluctuating.

4. If your bread is spongy and full of holes, perhaps you did not knead it for long enough. If it is very spongy, the dough was probably too wet. If it crumbles and falls apart, try adding more oil next time (some flours need more oil than others).

5. If the crust is pale and tough, the oven was not hot enough. If it is burnt on the crust and damp inside, the oven was too hot. If you don't succeed the first time, don't be discouraged. Flour types vary a lot and a little experience is necessary for tip-top results.

3 ¹/₂ **C** WHOLE WHEAT FLOUR

I t SALT

I ¹/₄ **C** MILK

I **T** FRESH YEAST, CREAMED WITH I t
  SUGAR

I **T** BUTTER

Bread Sticks

Makes about ten 8-inch sticks

Bread sticks may be made with
a portion of ordinary dough,
but a richer mixture is
probably better.

Sift flour and salt into a large
bowl and warm. Make a pocket
in the flower, add 2-3 T of the
milk to the creamed yeast and
pour the mixture in. Stir in 2-3
T of the flour and set in a warm
place to rise for about 20
minutes. Add remaining milk
warmed with the butter melted
into it. Now knead the dough
well for several minutes, then
leave to rise again, 10 minutes
or so. Cut dough into small
pieces and roll them out into
sticks 6 to 8 inches long and
no thicker than your little
finger. Leave in a warm place to
rise for 20 minutes, then they
can be twisted, plaited, or left
as they are, and baked at 350°
until crisp enough to snap in
two. Before baking, they can
also be brushed with milk and
sprinkled with rock salt, or
decorated with sesame, poppy,
or caraway seeds.

Soda Breads

Soda loaves are rich and crumbly. They are leavened with baking soda, and hence, require a cold environment and no kneading. Quick and easy to make, but it is believed that the baking soda destroys the B vitamins in the bread.

1 ¹/₂ **C** WHOLE WHEAT FLOUR
¹/₂ **t** BAKING POWDER
¹/₂ SALT
²/₃ **C** SOUR MILK OR BUTTERMILK

Irish Soda Farls
Makes one 8-inch diameter loaf

A good soda bread recipe for a camping trip, or whenever you need to make bread quickly without an oven.

Sift dry ingredients together. Knead in the buttermilk until the dough is soft, and turn onto a floured board. Roll out into a circle ¹/₄-inch thick and cut into quarters. Bake these on a medium hot floured griddle or cast-iron skillet for 2 ¹/₂ to 3 minutes on each side.

3 **C** WHOLE WHEAT FLOUR
1 **t** BAKING POWDER
³/₄ **t** SALT
1 ¹/₂ **C** BUTTERMILK

Irish Bannock
Makes one 7-inch diameter loaf

Sift the dry ingredients. Make a well in the mixture and stir in the buttermilk until the dough is firm. Shape into a 1-inch thick round on a floured board and turn it to coat both sides with flour. Place on an oiled tray and bake at 350° for 20 minutes.

2 MEDIUM-SIZED FRESHLY BOILED
  WHITE POTATOES

I t SALT

2 OZ ('/2 STICK) BUTTER

I C WHOLE WHEAT FLOUR

3 T MILK

'/2 t SAGE

'/2 t PAPRIKA

Irish Potato Cakes

Makes twelve 3-inch diameter cakes

Dry the potatoes well with a paper towel and mash them. Mix all ingredients together to form a stiff dough. Roll out 1/4-inch thick on a floured board. Cut into rounds. Bake the cakes on a medium hot floured griddle or heavy skillet for 2 1/2 to 3 minutes on each side. Serve hot with butter.

I '/2 C MEDIUM GROUND OATMEAL
  AND EXTRA FOR DUSTING

'/2 t SALT

'/2 t BAKING SODA

I OZ ('/4 STICK) BUTTER

'/2 C HOT WATER

Oatcakes

Makes twelve 3-inch diameter cakes

Oatcakes are delicious warm with butter and cheese, and also with a spreading of tahini. I have had some difficulty obtaining medium ground oatmeal. It is not the same as oat flour, but far coarser. You could try grinding whole oat berries at home to get the gritty texture needed for oatcakes if you can't find medium ground oatmeal.

Mix up dry ingredients. Melt butter into hot water and add it to the oatmeal mixture. Mix into a moist dough. On a board well dusted with oatmeal, roll out as thinly as possible to an even round, dusting with oatmeal to prevent sticking, and rubbing in more oatmeal with the palm of your hand. Cut into quarters or rounds and place on an ungreased baking tray. Bake the oatcakes at 350° for 20 minutes until they are crisp and golden.

2 **C** WHOLE WHEAT FLOUR
2 **C** CORNMEAL
2 **C** MILK OR BUTTERMILK
¹/₃ **C** WATER
2 ¹/₂ t BAKING POWDER
4 **T** OIL
4 **T** HONEY
2 **T** CORNSTARCH
PINCH OF SALT

Corn Bread
Makes one 9-inch diameter loaf

Blend all ingredients in a large mixing bowl. Pour into a 9-inch diameter cake pan and bake at 350° for about 30 minutes.

3 **C** CORNMEAL
1 **C** WHOLE WHEAT FLOUR
2 **C** MILK OR BUTTERMILK
¹/₂ **C** WATER
2 ¹/₂ t BAKING POWDER
4 **T** OIL
1 **T** FINELY CHOPPED FRESH CHILIS
2 t SALT

Mexican Corn Bread
Makes one 9-inch diameter loaf

A hotter, saltier corn bread.

Blend all ingredients in a large mixing bowl. Pour into a 9-inch diameter cake pan and bake at 350° for about 30 minutes.

3 **T** CUT MIXED PEEL OR 3 **T** CANDIED PEEL
3 **T** CURRANTS
5 OR 6 DRIED APRICOTS, STEWED UNTIL SOFT
3 **T** WALNUTS
5 **T** HONEY
1 ¹/₂ t MIXED SPICE (CINNAMON, CLOVES, ALLSPICE, AND NUTMEG)

Triipti's Fruit Bread
Makes 4 loaves

Make a bread dough (p. 146) using 10 ¹/₂ C whole wheat flour.

Now knead into the dough the ingredients.

Bake as for ordinary bread. When it's done, while still warm, brush the crust with a coating of warmed honey. Freezes well.

DOUGH:

4 ¹/₂ C WHOLE WHEAT FLOUR

1 T DRIED BAKER'S YEAST

1 TO 1 ¹/₄ C WARM MILK

4 OZ (1 STICK) BUTTER

¹/₂ C WARM WATER

2 T BROWN SUGAR

PINCH OF SALT

FILLING:

SOFT BROWN SUGAR OR SUCANAT

DOTS OF BUTTER

CHOPPED APPLE (SOUR VARIETIES
   ARE BEST)

SULTANAS OR OTHER DRIED FRUIT

FINELY CHOPPED BRAZIL NUTS OR
   OTHER NUTS

MIXED SPICE (FOR SPRINKLING);
   A COMBINATION OF CINNAMON,
   ALLSPICE, NUTMEG, AND CLOVES

Apfelstrudel

Makes one 16-inch long cake

Mix the yeast with the sugar. Pour warm water into this mixture and set in a warm place for about 15 minutes until frothy. Meanwhile, in a large bowl, rub the butter into the flour. Add yeast mixture and salt. Knead the mixture until it is soft and elastic, adding warm milk, until it is a soft, cushiony texture. Set the dough to rise for another 25 minutes. Now roll out the dough on a floured board into a large square about ¹/₄-inch thick. Cover the surface with a thin layer of sugar or sucanat and small dots of butter. Then add a sprinkling of chopped apple, some sultanas or other dried fruits, a sprinkling of finely chopped brazil nuts, and a sprinkling of mixed spice. Fold in the edges of the dough to stop the filling from rolling out, and roll up the pastry with the filling inside. Lift the strudel gently onto a baking tray, brush the surface with a little milk, and bake at 375° for about 30 minutes until firm. When it's done you can coat the crust with honey while it's still warm for a richer and stickier strudel. In Austria, the crust is coated with a layer of confectioner's sugar that has been boiled briefly in a small quantity of water to make a syrup, giving the strudel a festive appearance. This confection is a traditional Christmas treat.

PLAIN SCONES:

3 C WHOLE WHEAT PASTRY FLOUR (FINE)

³/₄ t BAKING POWDER

1 OZ (¹/₄ STICK) BUTTER

3 T SUGAR

1 ¹/₂ C BUTTERMILK

Scones

Makes eight 2 ¹/₂-inch diameter scones

Eat them for tea the same day with butter, raspberry jam, and cream. A pot of Earl Grey tea is the appropriate accompaniment.

Sift the flour and baking powder together and rub in the butter. Dissolve the sugar in the milk and mix all ingredients until smooth. Roll out on a floured board ³/₄-inch thick and cut into rounds. Brush the tops with milk. Bake at 350° for 12 to 15 minutes.

Variations:

Fruit and Nut Scones

Follow the above recipe, but mix with the flour 1 T raisins, 1 T currants, and 1 T chopped walnuts, or 1 ¹/₂ T dates and 1 T walnuts.

Herbed Cheese Scones

Substitute ²/₃ C grated cheddar cheese and ¹/₂ t salt for the sugar. Add ¹/₂ t each of sage, thyme, and marjoram. Bake 2 to 3 minutes longer than the plain ones.

1 **C** WHOLE WHEAT FLOUR
¹/₄ **t** BAKING POWDER
PINCH OF SALT
1 ¹/₄ **C** MILK
OIL FOR FRYING

Pancakes

Makes ten to fifteen 6- to 8-inch diameter pancakes

Pancakes are very versatile. They are nice to wrap vegetables in and serve with cheese sauce. Or rolled around a banana, with some syrup and lemon juice. Good with jam and cream too.

Sift dry ingredients together and stir in the milk to form a smooth, creamy batter. Leave to stand 15 to 30 minutes.

Heat up enough oil to cover the bottom of a heavy frying pan or griddle. Pour a ladleful of batter onto the griddle. Tilt the pan to thin the batter. Brown carefully, and make sure it doesn't stick with the aid of a spatula. Turn and brown the other side.

Store on a warm plate in a warm oven until you have enough to use.

Chapter 12

Cakes, Cookies, and Breakfast Dishes

It is easy to make delicious cakes without using eggs. You can have fun with cakes, and it is possible to use fruit, nuts, and spices in great variety. These recipes are just a few suggestions — as always, you're the cook. A recipe for a basic cake mix is followed by a series of simple variations.

Basic Cake Mix
Makes one 8-inch diameter cake

4 OZ (I STICK) BUTTER
I t VANILLA IF NO OTHER
   FLAVORINGS ARE TO BE ADDED
2/3 C SOFT BROWN SUGAR OR
   SUCANAT®
2 C WHOLE WHEAT FLOUR
I t BAKING POWDER
I 1/2 C MILK

Cream the butter, vanilla and sugar together. Sift the flour and baking powder together and mix them with the butter and sugar. Stir in the milk, and beat the mixture until it's smooth. Pour into an oiled 8-inch diameter cake pan and bake at 350° for at least 25 minutes, or until cake is springy and not sticking to the side of the pan.

Date and Walnut Cake
Makes one 8-inch diameter cake

TO BASIC CAKE MIX (ABOVE), ADD:
2 1/2 T CHOPPED DATES
2 T WALNUTS
I t CINNAMON
JUICE AND PEEL OF 1/2 LEMON (USE
   ONLY THE YELLOW PART OF THE
   PEEL, GRATED FINELY)

Prepare as for Basic Cake Mix.

BASIC CAKE MIX (P. 160) WITH
ONLY ¹/₂ C MILK
2 LARGE RIPE MASHED BANANAS
¹/₂ t GROUND CARDAMOM
¹/₂ t GROUND GINGER
I t VANILLA

Banana Cake

Makes one 8-inch diameter
cake

Follow the basic method,
adding the cardamom, ginger,
and vanilla to the basic mix,
but mix in the mashed banana
at the same time as the milk.
Bake at 325° for 40 minutes or
until firm and golden.

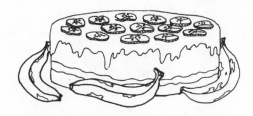

BASIC CAKE MIX (P. 160)
2 T WALNUTS
3 T FLAVORED INSTANT
   "INTERNATIONAL COFFEE" OR
   COFFEE SUBSTITUTE

FROSTING:
¹/₂ STICK BUTTER
I ¹/₃ C CONFECTIONER'S SUGAR
2 T FLAVORED INSTANT
   "INTERNATIONAL COFFEE" OR
   COFFEE SUBSTITUTE
WALNUTS FOR DECORATION

Coffee Walnut Cake

Makes one 8-inch diameter
cake

Follow the recipe for Basic Cake
Mix, adding the coffee essence and
walnuts to the basic mix. For the
frosting, soften the butter to a
creamy consistency and work in
the confectioner's sugar until a
smooth paste is obtained.
Continue blending, adding the
coffee essence, until the color and
texture of the frosting is uniform.
When the cake is cool, dip a
broad-blade knife into hot water
and use it to spread the frosting
evenly over the surface of the cake.
Decorate with pieces of walnut.

BASIC CAKE MIX (P. 160)
1 T DESICCATED COCONUT

Plain Coconut Cake
Makes one 8-inch diameter cake

Follow the method for Basic
Cake Mix, adding the coconut
at the same time as the flour.

BASIC CAKE MIX (P. 160)
3 LARGE BAKING APPLES, GRATED
2 OZ CHOPPED DATES
1 t CINNAMON
JUICE AND GRATED PEEL OF 1 LEMON

Date and Apple Cake
Makes one 8-inch diameter
cake

Follow the recipe for the Basic
Cake Mix, adding apple, dates,
lemon, and cinnamon with the
flour. Bake at 350° until firm
and golden (it could take up to
1 hour). This is a moist cake
with a rich flavor.

BASIC CAKE MIX (P. 160) USING
  APPLE JUICE INSTEAD OF MILK
$2/3$ t CINNAMON
$3/4$ TO $2/3$ C RAISINS

TOPPING:
2 TO 3 SOUR APPLES, GRATED OR
  DICED
1 $1/2$ T RAISINS
1 T BROWN SUGAR
PINCH GROUND CLOVES
$1/2$ C WATER
$1/2$ T CORNSTARCH, DISSOLVED IN A
  LITTLE COLD WATER

Applesauce Raisin Cake
Makes one 8-inch diameter
cake

Follow the recipe for Basic
Cake Mix, adding raisins and
spice with the flour. When the
cake is baked and cooled, make
the topping as follows.

Stew the apples, raisins, sugar,
and spice in the water until the
apples are soft. If the topping is
not thick enough, dissolve the
cornstarch in a little cold water
and add it to the apple mixture,
stirring all the time, until the
apple thickens. Spread this over
the top of the cake when cool.

BASIC CAKE MIX (P. 160)
3 T COCOA

FROSTING:
USE NUTELLA® CHOCOLATE
HAZELNUT SPREAD

Chocolate Cake

Makes one 8-inch diameter cake.

BASIC CAKE MIX (P. 160)
2 T DESICCATED COCONUT
2 T THICK, DARK MOLASSES

Coconut Treacle Cake

Makes one 8-inch diameter cake

Follow the recipe for Basic Cake Mix, adding the coconut and molasses with the flour. Decorate the top with a sprinkling of coconut. May need a little longer in the oven than the basic cake.

BASIC CAKE MIX (P. 160)
1 C DRIED APRICOTS
JUICE AND PEEL OF ¹/₂ LEMON (USE
ONLY YELLOW PART OF THE PEEL,
FINELY GRATED)

Apricot Cake

Makes one 8-inch diameter cake

Follow the recipe for Basic Cake Mix, adding the lemon after the wet ingredients. The apricots are stewed in a little water to achieve a thick, creamy consistency. You will need 2 to 4 C water and 10-20 minutes cooking time. Spread thickly on top of the cake when it is cool. This is a rich cake, good with cream.

CAKE:
BASIC CAKE MIX (P. 160)
3 T CAROB FLOUR, SIFTED WITH THE
   WHOLE WHEAT FLOUR

FUDGE:
1 ¹/₂ C SUGAR
2 OZ (¹/₂ STICK) BUTTER
1 T LIGHT CREAM
2 T CAROB POWDER

Carob Fudge Cake
Makes one 8-inch diameter cake

A rich, delicious cake.

To make the fudge:
Melt the butter and sugar together in a pan, stirring constantly with a wooden spoon. Add the cream and carob powder just a few moments later. Stir and boil the mixture gently until the sugar granules have dissolved and a drop of the mixture forms a soft ball when dropped into a saucer of cold water. Remove from the heat and beat the mixture for about 2-3 minutes, then pour it over the cake and leave to set. It's nice to decorate the top with walnuts.

Ginger Fudge Cake
Makes one 8-inch diameter cake

To Basic Cake Mix (p. 160), add 1 t ginger powder. Make a fudge, as in the recipe for Carob Fudge Cake, but instead of carob flour, use 1 t dry ginger powder.

CREAM CHEESE FROSTINGS

Try these frostings with cakes containing lots of dried fruit and nuts, and with carrot cake.

Honey and Cream Cheese Frosting
Makes enough for one 8-inch diameter cake

Mix 8 oz softened cream cheese with 3 T honey. Blend them together well, spread over your cake, and decorate with walnuts.

Banana Frosting
Makes enough for one 9- to 12-inch diameter cake

Mix 8 oz softened cream cheese with 3 T honey and the pulp of a ripe banana. Blend well together with a few drops of vanilla essence. This will discolor after a while, so spread just before ready to eat it.

Lemon Frosting
Makes enough for one 8- to 10-inch diameter cake

Mix 8 oz softened cream cheese with 3 T honey and the juice of 1 lemon.

6 OZ ('/2 STICK) BUTTER

'/3 **C** SOFT BROWN SUGAR

'/4 **C** HONEY

4 **C** SOFT ROLLED OATS

'/4 **C** FILBERTS, CHOPPED FINELY

'/4 **C** RAISINS

Honey Crunch

Makes enough for two 8-inch diameter shallow cake pans

Blend the butter, sugar, and honey together well. Mix in the oats, nuts, and raisins. Press the mixture into buttered shallow cake pans and bake at 275° for 25 to 30 minutes, until browned and firm. Cut into slices while hot, but eat it when cool.

8 OZ (2 STICKS) BUTTER

I **C** BROWN SUGAR

2 **T** HONEY

4 **C** ROLLED OATS

Flapjacks (Sweet Oatcakes)

Makes enough for two 8-inch diameter shallow cake pans

Melt the butter, sugar and honey together and add the oats. Pat the mixture into cake pans and bake at 350° for 20 to 30 minutes until golden. Cut into slices while hot, then leave to cool.

8 OZ (2 STICKS) BUTTER

I **C** BROWN SUGAR

2 **T** HONEY

4 **C** ROLLED OATS

I **T** CANDIED CHERRIES, CHOPPED

2 **T** WALNUTS, CHOPPED

2 **T** RAISINS

I BAR SWEET BAKING CHOCOLATE

Florentines

Makes enough for two 8-inch diameter shallow cake pans

Follow the instructions for Flapjacks (above), but add the fruit and nuts with the oats. Melt the chocolate in a double boiler and pour it over the baked oatcake while still hot. Cut in squares and allow to cool.

4 **C** SOFT ROLLED OATS

8 OZ (1 STICK) BUTTER

$^1/_2$ **C** HONEY

$^1/_2$ **t** CINNAMON

$^1/_4$ **t** POWDERED GINGER

1 **C** WATER

<u>FILLING:</u>

1 $^1/_2$ **C** CHOPPED DATES OR
    APRICOTS

JUICE AND GRATED RIND (YELLOW
    PART ONLY) OF $^1/_2$ LEMON

1 **t** CINNAMON

1 **C** WATER

Apricot or Date Layer Cake

Makes one 8-inch x 12-inch cake

Stew the dates gently in water with the lemon and cinnamon, until soft and thick. Melt the butter and stir in the oats and honey. Add water until the mixture is no longer quite so crumbly, and holds together a little. Spread out half of the oatmeal mixture $^1/_2$-inch thick in an 8-inch x 12-inch oiled baking pan, and press it down. Spread all the stewed dates in an even layer over the surface. Press the rest of the oatmeal mixture evenly over the dates and bake the cake at 350° for 25 to 30 minutes.

1 $^3/_4$ **C** WHITE FLOUR

4 OZ (1 STICK) BUTTER

$^2/_3$ **C** SOFT BROWN SUGAR

1 **t** GROUND DRY GINGER

1 **T** THICK, DARK MOLASSES

1 **T** HONEY

JUICE OF SMALL ORANGE OR SOME
    MARMALADE TO HELP MAKE THE
    MIXTURE WORKABLE

Gingerbread People

Makes eighteen 3-inch cookies

Rub the butter into the flour. Mix the sugars and the ginger all together and stir them into the flour. When it's all well-mixed, add the orange juice or marmalade. Roll out the dough on a floured board and cut it into rounds or shapes. (Use raisins for the eyes, mouth, and buttons.) Bake the cookies on a greased and floured tray at 350° for about 10 minutes. Remove from the tray with a spatula and place on a wire rack to cool.

1 **C** CURRANTS
1 **C** SULTANAS (GOLDEN RAISINS)
3 OZ (³/₄ STICK) BUTTER
1 t CINNAMON
¹/₂ t GINGER POWDER
1 t MACE
1 **C** SOFT BROWN SUGAR
1 **C** WARM WATER
3 **T** MILK
2 **C** WHOLE WHEAT FLOUR
2 t BAKING POWDER

Jyoti's Fruit Cake
Makes 1 large loaf

Put the dried fruit, butter, spice, and sugar in a pan with the water and simmer gently for 10 minutes to let the fruit swell. Allow to cool. Add milk. Now sift the flour and baking powder together and add them to the fruit mixture, mixing it all together well. Pour into two loaf tins and bake at 350° for 15 minutes and then at 325° for about 45 minutes. Cool, cut into slices and eat with butter.

¹/₂ **C** SOFT BROWN SUGAR
1 ¹/₂ t MIXED SPICE
2 ¹/₂ t GROUND GINGER
4 **C** WHOLE WHEAT FLOUR
4 OZ (1 STICK) BUTTER
4 **T** HONEY
5 **T** THICK, DARK MOLASSES
2 **C** MILK
2 t BAKING SODA
CRYSTALLIZED GINGER TO DECORATE

Gloucestershire Ginger Cake
Makes 2 medium loaves

Mix the sugar, spices, and flour together in a bowl. In a pan, melt the butter and add the honey and molasses. Stir until dissolved. Warm the milk separately and dissolve the soda in it, then combine the liquid ingredients. Add them to the flour and mix all together well, then pour it into well-oiled loaf pans. Bake at 300° for 50 minutes or until firm. When cool, brush the crust with warm honey and decorate with slices of crystallized ginger.

1 **C** HONEY, OR 1/2 **C** HONEY AND
  1/2 **C** BROWN SUGAR
1 **C** MILK
3 OZ (3/4 STICK) BUTTER
2 1/2 **C** UNBLEACHED WHOLE WHEAT
  PASTRY FLOUR
PINCH OF SALT
1 t BAKING POWDER
1/2 **C** WALNUTS (OR MORE)
1 t CINNAMON
1 t GINGER GROUND

Honey Walnut Bread

Makes 1 loaf

Heat honey, milk, and butter together until they are blended. Sift together all the dry ingredients and combine them with the wet mixture. Pour into an oiled loaf pan and bake 50 to 60 minutes at 350°. Allow to cool in the pan for 15 minutes before removing, and then let it cool before cutting. Slice and serve with butter.

1 2/3 **C** DESICCATED COCONUT
1/2 **C** SOFT BROWN SUGAR
1 t GROUND GINGER
2 **C** WHOLE WHEAT PASTRY FLOUR
1 PINCH OF SALT
1 t BAKING POWDER
1 **C** MILK

Coconut Loaf

Makes 1 medium loaf

Sift dry ingredients together and stir in the milk. Pour the mixture into a small buttered loaf pan. Bake about 45 minutes at 300° until firm.

4 oz (1 STICK) BUTTER

1 C MILK

¹/₂ C BROWN SUGAR

2 C GRATED CARROTS

¹/₂ t CINNAMON

¹/₂ t POWDERED GINGER

1 C WHOLE WHEAT FLOUR

1 C OAT FLOUR

1 t BAKING POWDER

Carrot Cake
Makes one 8-inch diameter cake

Melt the butter in a saucepan with the milk and sugar. Combine the carrots, spices, flours, and baking powder in a large mixing bowl, and when the milk is hot and the butter melted, pour the milk mixture into the bowl. Blend all ingredients well. Transfer to an oiled cake pan and bake at 325° for about 30 minutes.

2 C WHOLE WHEAT FLOUR

¹/₂ t SALT

¹/₂ t GROUND MACE

2 t CINNAMON

2 t BAKING POWDER

5 oz. (1 ¹/₄ STICKS) BUTTER

¹/₂ C BROWN SUGAR OR HONEY

¹/₂ C MILK

1 C CHOPPED DATES

¹/₂ C CHOPPED WALNUTS

2 t GRATED ORANGE RIND (COLORED PART ONLY)

Date and Walnut Bread
Makes 1 large loaf

Sift together the flour, salt, spices, and baking powder. Cream together the butter and sugar and add the dry ingredients gradually with milk. Mix in the dates, nuts, and orange rind. Turn into a greased loaf pan and bake approximately 1 hour at 325°. Allow it to cool before you remove it from the pan.

½ C BROWN SUGAR
4 OZ (I STICK) BUTTER
I C WHOLE WHEAT FLOUR
I ½ C SOFT ROLLED OATS
I t HONEY
I T WARM WATER
¼ t BAKING SODA

Suttie's Cookies

Makes about fifteen 3-inch cookies

My grandmother's recipe.

Cream together the sugar and the butter. Add the flour and oats. Melt the honey in a pan with the warm water and into this dissolve baking soda. Mix this with the other ingredients until all ingredients are well-blended. Roll a small piece of the mixture into a ball about the size of a small egg. On a wooden board, squash it down as thinly as possible. With a spatula, transfer the cookies to an oiled baking tray. Bake them at 375° for 10 minutes or until golden. Slide them from the tray with the spatula and leave to crisp on a wire rack. After 5 minutes you will have thin, crispy cookies.

Hazelnut Cookies

Make these in exactly the same way as the recipe for Suttie's Cookies. Together with the oats and flour, add 1 C filberts or hazelnuts, roasted and finely ground. Add a little extra water to make the mixture sufficiently damp.

8 OZ (2 STICKS) BUTTER
I C SUGAR
I 1/2 C WHOLE WHEAT PASTRY FLOUR
1/4 C WHITE RICE FLOUR

Shortbread

Makes one 8-inch diameter tray

My mother's recipe — very rich.

Cream butter and sugar and fold in flours. Press into a shallow, circular 8-inch cake pan and prick with a fork to decorate. Bake at 300° for 15 to 20 minutes. Cut into triangles while hot. Allow to cool (it will harden when cool).

6 T HONEY
3/4 C PEANUT BUTTER
1/2 C DESICCATED COCONUT
I C SESAME SEEDS
I C MILK POWDER

No-bake Sesame Seed Squares

Makes 15-18 small squares

Melt the honey gently and mix in the peanut butter. Add coconut, sesame seeds, and milk powder. Mix well and press into a tin and cut in squares. Refrigerate for a while to make it firm.

4 OZ (I STICK) BUTTER
1/2 C SOFT BROWN SUGAR
2 T MILK
1 3/4 C WHOLE WHEAT PASTRY FLOUR
SOME WHOLE ALMONDS TO
    DECORATE

Egyptian Cookies

Makes about sixteen 2 1/2-inch cookies

Cream together the butter and sugar, then mix in milk and then flour. Squash small handfuls into cookie shapes and decorate each one with an almond in the middle. Bake at 375° for about 10 minutes until browned.

6 OZ (1 ¹/₂ STICKS) BUTTER
1 C BROWN SUGAR
1 T HONEY
2 ²/₃ C SOFT OATS
1 C DESICCATED COCONUT

Coconut Oaties

Makes enough for one 8-inch diameter shallow cake pan

Melt the butter, sugar, and honey together then stir in the oats and coconut. Spread the mixture in a buttered cake pan and bake at 375° for 20 minutes. Cut while hot, then leave to cool.

4 OZ (1 STICK) BUTTER
1 C BROWN SUGAR
1 C SUGAR
1 t VANILLA
1 C WHOLE WHEAT FLOUR
1 ¹/₂ C OAT FLOUR
²/₃ C UNBLEACHED PASTRY FLOUR
¹/₃ C CORNSTARCH
1 t BAKING POWDER
1 t BAKING SODA
PINCH OF SALT
1 C MILK
¹/₂ C CHOCOLATE CHIPS
1 ¹/₂ C CHOPPED NUTS
1 ¹/₂ t GRATED ORANGE PEEL
  (COLORED PART ONLY)

Biscake

Makes one 10-inch x 15-inch baking pan

Cream butter, sugar and vanilla. Mix in flours, cornstarch, baking powder, soda and salt. Mix in milk. Add chocolate and nuts with orange peel. Pour into a shallow well-oiled 10-inch x 15-inch baking pan and bake at 325° for 10 to 15 minutes or until golden and risen. Cool slightly before cutting into squares. You may need to slide a spatula under the squares to lift them out of the tray.

Jam Roly-poly

Roll leftover pie crust into a ¹/₄-inch thick oblong sheet. Spread with a generous layer of jam, roll up the pastry and bake it on a cookie sheet at 350° until firm. Cut into slices and pour evaporated milk on top. This is very heavy, and popular with hungry children in winter.

Puddings and Desserts

Factory-made confectionery and baked goods are often excessively sweetened and full of preservatives and other chemicals. Any homemade desserts can be made far nicer and more wholesome by using whole grains, fresh fruits and their natural sweetness, and some honey in addition to or instead of sugar.

The following recipes contain these ingredients and are vegetarian, and so do not use eggs or gelatin. Gelatin is taken from calves hooves and used to make jellies and molds. The vegetarian substitute is agar-agar, a white powder extracted from seaweed. It can be bought from a good herbalist or health food store. Some health food stores also stock vegetarian jell mix made with natural color and flavorings.

About Custard

Custard is a vanilla-flavored dessert sauce and can be served hot or cold. In the United States the best brand, Bird's Custard®, can sometimes be obtained from good delicatessens.

A Dutch brand, Honig®, is also available in well-stocked supermarkets.

Baked Apples
Serves 4

4 LARGE TART APPLES

STUFFING 1:
1 C RAISINS
1 C WATER
JUICE OF 1 LEMON
PINCH GROUND CLOVES
1/2 t CINNAMON
3 T RASPBERRY JAM

STUFFING 2:
(AN ALTERNATIVE APPLE STUFFING)
1/2 C CHOPPED DATES
1/2 TO 2/3 C WATER
JUICE OF 1 LEMON
1/2 t CINNAMON
1/2 C CHOPPED WALNUTS

Stew the dried fruits gently in the water with the lemon and spice until the water is absorbed. Meanwhile, wash and core the apples and score them around the waist to stop them bursting. Add the nuts or jam to the fruit and force it down the center of each apple, pouring any surplus water over the apples. Bake them at 350° for 15 to 20 minutes. Make some custard while the apples are baking.

16 DRIED APRICOTS
1 C WATER
3 C MILK
4 T SUGAR
4 T CORNSTARCH
GRATED RIND AND JUICE OF A LEMON
HONEY FOR EXTRA SWEETENING

Lemon Apricot Blancmange
Serves 4

Cover the dried apricots with water and simmer them 15 minutes until very soft. Blend until smooth with 1 C milk in a blender. Heat 1 ½ C milk in a separate pan. Dissolve the sugar and cornstarch in the remaining milk in a big bowl. When the milk is almost boiling, pour it onto the mixture, stirring it, and then return all the mixture to the pan and reheat. Stir constantly until the cornstarch thickens. Add the apricot purée. Add the lemon and mix well. Sweeten with honey if you like. Transfer the blancmange to a mold or dish and leave to set.

**2 OR 3 BRAMLEYS OR OTHER TART
APPLES
2 C BLACKBERRIES
A THIN SPRINKLING OF BROWN SUGAR
I t CINNAMON**

**CRUMBLE:
2 ¹/₂ C WHOLE WHEAT FLOUR,
4 OZ (I STICK) BUTTER AND
¹/₂ C SUGAR, RUBBED TOGETHER**

Blackberry and Apple Crumble

Serves 4

Wash and slice the apples and clean the berries. Arrange them in a buttered deep-dish pie pan or cake pan and sprinkle with sugar and cinnamon. Make the crumble and spread it over the top and bake at 350° until it is brown and crispy.

**2 C RHUBARB, SLICED ¹/₂-INCH THICK
SOFT BROWN SUGAR FOR SPRINKLING
I t CINNAMON**

**CRUMBLE:
2 ¹/₂ C WHOLE WHEAT FLOUR,
4 OZ (I STICK) BUTTER AND ¹/₂ C
SUGAR, RUBBED TOGETHER**

Rhubarb Crumble

Serves 4

Wash and slice the rhubarb. Spread it in the bottom of a buttered deep-dish pie pan or cake pan, and sprinkle with sugar and cinnamon. Make the crumble and spread on top. Bake at 350° until brown and crisp.

**3 C GOOSEBERRIES
ABOUT ¹/₃ C HONEY OR SUGAR
   (AMOUNT DEPENDS ON SOURNESS
   OF GOOSEBERRIES)
³/₄ C THICK CREAM**

Gooseberry Fool

Serves 4-6

Top and tail the gooseberries and stew them very gently in a little water until soft. Mix in enough honey or sugar to sweeten them. Blend with the cream. Cool and serve in small individual dishes.

I lb GOOSEBERRIES
HONEY TO TASTE

Gooseberry Tart

Make a rich pastry crust (p. 66) and line a tart tin with it. Brown the pastry a little at 325°. Top and tail the gooseberries and stew them gently in a little water until soft. Sweeten them with honey. Pour the gooseberries into the pastry and lattice the top of the tart with leftover pieces. Bake at 350° until the pastry browns. Serve with custard or cream.

Note:
For gooseberry recipes, elder flowers add an interesting subtle flavor. For every 2 C gooseberries, throw in a spray of elder flowers while stewing them. Leave in for just a few minutes, then discard.

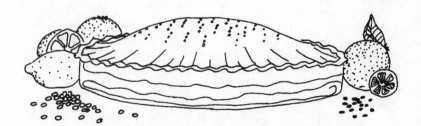

CRUMB CRUST:

2 **C** CRUSHED GRAHAM CRACKERS

3 **T** BUTTER

2 **T** SOFT BROWN SUGAR

FILLING:

I **lb** COTTAGE CHEESE

JUICE OF 2 MEDIUM SIZED ORANGES
   PLUS ¹/₂ **t** OF THE FINELY GRATED
   ORANGE PEEL (USE COLORED PART
   ONLY)

3 **T** SOFT BROWN SUGAR

I **t** POWDERED AGAR AGAR

Orange Cheesecake
Serves 6-8

A light cheesecake made with low-fat cottage cheese. The taste is orangey and not too sweet.

Crush the graham crackers with a rolling pin. Melt the butter and sugar together over a low heat and stir the crumbs in, kneading a little to blend well. Press the crust into the bottom of a 9-inch diameter glass dish and refrigerate it while you make the filling. For this, blend the cottage cheese in an electric blender with the peel and juice of the oranges. In a small saucepan dissolve the sugar and agar-agar and heat to boiling, stirring constantly. It will thicken. Continue stirring for 1 minute, then quickly pour into the blender and blend with the cheese and orange. Pour this mixture over the crust and return it to the refrigerator for about 30 minutes to set. Delicious, but eat within one or two days, or the crust will become soggy.

2 C DRIED PRUNES
JUICE OF 2 ORANGES
2 T HONEY
¹/₂ C SOUR CREAM
2 C WATER

Prune Fool

Serves 4-6

Stew the prunes gently in water. When soft, take out the stones and purée the prunes with the other ingredients. Pour into small glass dishes, chill, and serve.

1 ¹/₂ C RASPBERRIES
1 ¹/₂ C BLUEBERRIES
ABOUT ¹/₂ C WATER
3 TO 4 T SUGAR OR HONEY (MORE OR LESS DEPENDING ON HOW SOUR THE FRUIT IS)
FEW SLICES OF SOFT WHITE BREAD WITH CRUSTS REMOVED

Summer Pudding

Serves 4-6

Stew the fruit very gently with the sweetening in water until it is soft. Soak the bread in the fruit juice for a few minutes. Butter a pudding dish, and line it with slices of bread. Pour the fruit into the middle of the basin and top with a slice of bread to cover the fruit. Place a small plate on top of the pudding and weigh it down with something heavy so that the pudding will be compressed. Refrigerate. After 24 hours, uncover the pudding and turn it gently onto a plate. Serve with cream or yogurt.

English Trifle

Trifle is traditional in England for family festivals and rites of passage, such as weddings and birthdays. It is made from stale sponge cake, traditionally soaked in brandy, sherry, or rum and topped with layers of fruit, jell, custard, and cream and then decorated with chopped nuts. Trifles with plenty of liquor soaked in are frequently called "tipsy" trifles, but the following version will allow you to drive home safely. You need never make the same trifle twice, since the cake, fruits, and jellies used will vary with the season.

Trifle
Serves 6-10

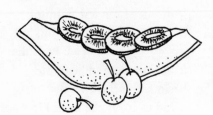

Break up a stale vanilla or almond-flavored sponge cake and lay the pieces in the bottom of a big flat-bottomed bowl. Pour some fruit juice (orange or grapefruit) over the cake. For extra flavor, add the juice of half a lime. Leave the cake to soak. Make a vegetarian jell — any flavor — according to the instructions on the package, or with agar-agar, adding some fruit. Orange sections, slices of apple and pear, fresh, frozen or canned strawberries, pineapple, raspberries, and peaches are good. Pour the jell over the cake and leave it to set. Refrigerate. Meanwhile, make up some custard (p. 174), adding slices of fresh bananas. Pour the custard over the jell when it sets. Finally, decorate the top of the trifle with chopped nuts and whipped cream. Chill it in the fridge. Now find someone with a birthday to celebrate!

SEVERAL SLICES OF STALE BREAD,
BUTTERED, WITH THE CRUSTS
CUT OFF
MILK
SUGAR (VERY DARK BROWN IS BEST)
A FEW RAISINS
FINELY GRATED LEMON RIND: ABOUT
   $1/2$ LEMON FOR EVERY **2 C** MILK
PINCH OF NUTMEG

Bread and Butter Pudding

A favorite pudding to use up your stale bread.

Tear the bread into large pieces in a buttered oven dish and cover well with milk. Stir in sugar to taste and a handful of raisins. Add the lemon rind and a little freshly grated nutmeg. Leave the pudding to soak for a few hours until it gets very mushy; then bake at 350° 25 to 30 minutes until browned and set.

2 C THICK CUSTARD (P. 174)
I C CREAM
3 VERY RIPE BANANAS
NUTS TO DECORATE
$1/4$ t NUTMEG

Banana Cream Whip
Serves 8

Blend all ingredients in a blender. Alternatively, mash the bananas and whisk them well into the custard and cream. Pour the mixture into individual dishes and decorate with chopped nuts.

5 C MILK

2 T SHORT GRAIN BROWN RICE

2 T SOFT BROWN SUGAR OR HONEY

¹/₈ t NUTMEG

¹/₈ t CRUSHED CARDAMOM SEED

¹/₄ STICK BUTTER

Rice Pudding
Serves 5

Heat milk in a saucepan. Put the rice (yes, only 2T!), sugar, spice, and butter in a large buttered casserole dish that has a tightly fitting lid. Pour boiling milk onto the rice. Cover and bake at 175° for at least 2 hours.

4 T SOFT BROWN SUGAR OR HONEY

²/₃ C COLD WATER

¹/₂ T AGAR-AGAR

¹/₄ t VANILLA

1 ¹/₂ C THICK PLAIN YOGURT

¹/₂ C THICK CREAM OR SOUR CREAM

3 C CHOPPED MIXED FRESH FRUIT

  (PINEAPPLE, STRAWBERRIES, KIWI

  FRUIT, BANANA, GRAPES, CHERRIES,

  MANDARIN ORANGE)

¹/₂ t GRATED RIND OF TANGERINE OR

  MANDARIN ORANGE (USE COLORED

  PART ONLY)

Ambrosia
Serves 5

Put the sugar, water, agar-agar, and vanilla in a saucepan, and blend the agar-agar into the water. Gently heat to boiling, stirring constantly, and simmer for 1 minute until well thickened. Mix in the yogurt and cream, and beat until smooth. Add the fruit and tangerine peel and mix well. Pour into a large glass bowl and refrigerate until set.

2 **C** RAISINS

I **C** SULTANAS OR CURRANTS

2 APPLES, GRATED

2 t POWDERED GINGER

2 **C** BREAD CRUMBS

$^1/_2$ **C** GROUND ALMONDS

2 LARGE CARROTS

3 **T** MIXED PEEL (A MIXTURE OF
CANDIED ORANGE AND LEMON PEEL)

3 **T** FRESH ORANGE JUICE

2 t ORANGE RIND (COLORED PART
ONLY)

I t INSTANT "INTERNATIONAL
COFFEE" OR SWEETENED COFFEE
SUBSTITUTE

2 t CINNAMON

No-bake Christmas Pudding
Serves 8-10

Mix together dried fruit, grated apple, and ginger. Then mix all the other ingredients and press the mixture down firmly into a buttered basin. Keep refrigerated overnight with a weight on top. This is a light, refreshing Christmas pudding which is enriched if served with whipped cream!

$^3/_4$ **C** DRIED APRICOTS

2 **C** DRIED APPLES

$^3/_4$ **C** DATES

$^3/_4$ **C** RAISINS

$^3/_4$ **C** SUNFLOWER SEEDS

I $^1/_2$ **C** NUTS

ORANGE JUICE

DESICCATED COCONUT

Energy Balls
Makes 15-20 small balls

Blend or grind the dried fruits and nuts together in a mincer. Add enough fresh orange juice to form the mixture into moist balls. Roll them in desiccated coconut to make little sweets. They make a nice present for birthdays, etc.

Breakfast

Breakfast sets the scene for the day. It should be fresh, light, and easy to eat. It is the first meal of the day, so prepare it with extra love and care and eat it in a peaceful, relaxed environment.

MAKING YOUR OWN YOGURT

Homemade yogurt is mild and creamy and much more economical than good-quality store brands. Here are the steps to making your own:

1. If using raw or pasteurized milk, it must first be heated almost to boiling point to kill little organisms in the milk that would interfere with the growth of the yogurt culture. If using sterilized or evaporated milk, it is only necessary to warm it to lukewarm.

2. Pour the milk into a clean, dry container, preferably one that holds heat well (plastic is good); do not use metal. Leave it to cool until lukewarm.

3. Mix the culture with a little of the warm milk in a cup, and then mix this back into the rest of the milk again. The culture can be specially bought, or with equally good results you can use a tablespoon of live natural yogurt.

4. Put the container in a warm place where the milk will not go cold for several hours: in the airing cupboard or near the pilot light on a gas stove, for instance, (with a rack or pan underneath to protect the plastic). Wrap it in a towel to keep it warm. Leave it alone for several hours or overnight, so the yogurt bacteria can grow and thicken the milk. When it has thickened to yogurt consistency, halt the process by putting the container in a colder place. Yogurt that is left for too long tends to separate into curds and whey. Six hours is usually about right.

Note: For thicker, creamier yogurt, try adding a few teaspoons of milk powder to the milk before adding the culture, or mix fresh milk with undiluted evaporated milk. You can make yogurt at night and leave it to thicken for breakfast, saving a little from each batch as a culture for the next batch. Take care that the starter you use is always sweet-tasting and good, not sour and fizzy. If your yogurt fails to thicken, maybe it's because:

a. The milk was too cold or too hot when starter was added
b. The place where it "yogged" wasn't warm enough
c. The culture was no longer good

When your yogurt is ready, it can be eaten without any further delay. If you don't like plain yogurt, try using it in the following recipes. Invent your own flavorings using different fruits, nuts and spices.

I **C** DRIED APRICOTS
2 **C** YOGURT
HONEY TO TASTE

Apricot Yogurt
Serves 2-6

Stew the apricots in a little water until soft. Blend them with the yogurt and add honey if you want it a little sweeter.

I TO 2 APPLES, GRATED
2 **C** YOGURT
¹/₂ t CINNAMON
HONEY TO TASTE

Apple Yogurt
Serves 2-6

Blend the apples into the yogurt, cinnamon and honey. If you don't have a blender, stew the apples into a purée and allow to cool before mixing with the other ingredients. Add some finely chopped nuts if desired.

I TO 2 BANANAS
2 **C** YOGURT
FEW DROPS VANILLA
HONEY TO TASTE

Banana Yogurt
Serves 2-6

Mash bananas. Mix ingredients together.

Yogurt Cheese

Hang one or two pints of yogurt in a piece of fine cotton or muslin or a clean tea towel and let the liquid drip for 12 hours or so. This cheese is really tasty if mixed with honey, fresh fruits, and chopped nuts.

Ananda Loka Muesli

Take a bowl large enough for the number of people the muesli is to serve, and fill it to halfway with unflavored yogurt. Stir in some soft rolled oats, enough to make the mixture the texture of thick cream. Add some dried fruits which have soaked overnight and are soft and sweet — try figs, dates, apricots, raisins, or prunes. A handful of nuts goes in next, and some lemon juice. A pinch of powdered vanilla is delicious. The muesli should now be left to soak for an hour or two if possible. Before serving it, chop in a banana or two and grate in enough apples to fill the bowl.

Yogi Breakfast

Chop up as many different kinds of fresh fruit as are in season in a bowl. Add some nuts and cover with creamy yogurt.

Cooked Cereals

If you like hot, filling breakfasts, oat or wheat porridge is good, but there are also other cereals to choose from:

2 ¹/₂ C WATER
2 T SMALL PEARL TAPIOCA
¹/₂ C EVAPORATED MILK
2 T HONEY

Tapioca
Serves 2-3

Heat water with tapioca. Simmer and cook the tapioca slowly for about 15 minutes, stir often. Add honey and evaporated milk. Cook 1 minute longer.

2 ¹/₂ C MILK
3 ¹/₂ T WHOLE WHEAT SEMOLINA
STEWED PRUNES OR STEWED DATES AND/OR APPLE PIECES (OPTIONAL)

Semolina
Serves 2-3

Heat milk in a saucepan and stir in semolina when milk is warm. Stir constantly until thick. It takes about 5 minutes. Sweeten to taste.

2 C SOFT ROLLED OAT FLAKES
2 T OIL
2 T HONEY
I t VANILLA
I C MIXED CHOPPED ALMONDS, **HUNZA APRICOTS AND DESICCATED COCONUT**

Hunza Granola
Serves 4

Granola is a mixture of cereal flakes, honey, fruit, and nuts lightly roasted in oil. It can be bought ready-made, or can be made at home. Mix well. Scatter into a large, shallow oiled casserole dish. Bake at 350° for 5 minutes. Remove from oven, stir, bake 5 minutes more. It can be stored in an airtight jar and eaten for breakfast with milk.

1 C OAT FLAKES
½ C CHOPPED DATES
PINCH OF SALT
2 ½ C MILK AND WATER MIXED HALF-
  AND-HALF (1 ¼ C EACH)
⅓ C WALNUTS

Date and Walnut Porridge
Serves 2-3

Simmer the oats, dates, and salt together in the milk/water mixture for 5 minutes, stirring often. Add the nuts and stir a few seconds longer.

5 PARTS WHOLE WHEAT FLOUR TO TWO
  PARTS SEMOLINA
A LITTLE SALT
PINCH OF BAKING SODA
MILK
FRESH STRAWBERRIES
CREAM
HONEY FOR SYRUP
OIL FOR FRYING

Pancakes for Special Occasions

For us, this was a wedding breakfast for twenty people.

Mix together flour, semolina, salt, and soda. Gradually stir in enough milk to make a fine, creamy batter. Leave to stand while you wash strawberries, cut lemons, and make syrup. For syrup, dissolve honey in a little hot water; enough to make it liquid but still thick. Fry the pancakes on a hot griddle in plenty of oil; to fry, pour ½ ladle of batter evenly over the griddle. Let it cook for a few minutes, loosening the edges with a spatula to prevent sticking. Turn and brown the other side for only ½ to one minute. Store pancakes on a warm plate in the oven until there are enough. Serve with strawberries, cream, and syrup.

Chapter 13

Beverages

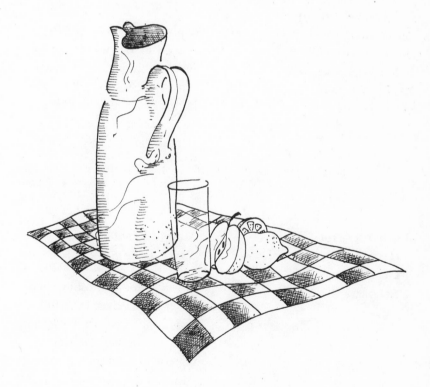

4 C WATER
8 WHITE CARDAMOM PODS
12 WHOLE BLACK PEPPERCORNS
6 WHOLE CLOVES
1 STICK CINNAMON
2 SLICES FRESH GINGER ROOT
5 STARS OF STAR ANISE

Yogi Tea
Serves 2

Bring to a boil and simmer covered for half an hour. Strain and drink hot. Very refreshing, and best taken in the late evening.

A FEW SPRAYS OF ELDER FLOWERS
   (ENOUGH SO THAT THE WATER
   JUST COVERS THEM)
2 ¹/₂ C WATER
JUICE OF 1 LEMON
1 T SUGAR OR HONEY

Elderflowerade
Serves 2

Gather the fragrant elder flowers in May when they are just beginning to open. Cover them with water, soak for 24 hours. Strain. Add lemon juice and sugar or honey to water. Heat to dissolve the sweetener. Serve cool.

1 C NATURAL YOGURT
1 C MANGO JUICE
1 C WATER
2 T SUGAR

Mango Lassi
Serves 3

Lassi is a cool, refreshing, and delicious beverage from India, consisting of yogurt, water, and various other sweet or salty ingredients, depending on season and taste.

Blend together.

1 **C** NATURAL YOGURT
2 **C** WATER
3 **T** SUGAR
1 **t** ROSEWATER

Rosewater Lassi
Serves 2

Blend together.

1 **C** MILK
1 **t** HONEY
¹/₄ **t** GROUND GINGER

Ginger Milk
Serves 1

Warm in a pan. A warming
drink on cold nights.

Herb Teas

Herb teas are made in exactly the same way as ordinary teas if the leaves of the plant are used. Herb teas need to be left to brew a little longer: 5 to 10 minutes. Try spearmint, peppermint, lemon verbena, or chamomile to begin with. When you are used to these, try nettle, raspberry leaf, lemon thyme, lime (linden) flower. Some types of seeds can be made into teas. Pour boiling water onto the seeds, using the same amount of seeds as you would ordinary tea leaves. Boil for a few minutes in a saucepan to bring out the flavor. Try rose hips, fennel seeds, anise seeds.

2 ¹/₂ C WATER
JUICE OF 1 LEMON
¹/₂ t SEA SALT OR ¹/₄ t TABLE SALT

Lemon Water

Serves 2

This drink cleanses the blood and is very refreshing. If you are in the habit of fasting regularly, this drink helps clean the body and neutralizes acid digestive juices in the stomach. It is also a very good drink first thing in the morning.

Mix and drink.

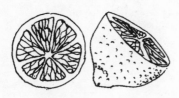

MILK SHAKES

2 C MILK
¹/₂ BANANA
I T HONEY
PINCH OF NUTMEG
PINCH OF CINNAMON

Honey Banana Shake
Serves 2

Blend

2 C MILK
¹/₂ C STRAWBERRIES
I T SUGAR OR HONEY

Strawberry Shake
Serves 2

Blend

2 C MILK
¹/₂ T SWEETENED INSTANT **COFFEE**
  OR COFFEE SUBSTITUTE
2 T SUGAR
2 T COCOA

Mocha Shake
Serves 2

Blend

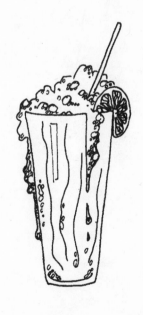

4 CLOVES, FINELY CRUSHED
4 T BROWN SUGAR
1 ¹/₂ C WATER
1 ¹/₂ C MILK
¹/₂ C COCONUT MILK

Coconut Clove Shake
Serves 3

Heat cloves with sugar and water in a saucepan and simmer, covered, for 5 minutes. Blend with milk and coconut milk. Serve warm or chill.

2 C CHOPPED PITTED WATERMELON
2 T SUGAR OR HONEY
1 t ROSEWATER
2 C MILK

Watermelon Shake
Serves 2

Blend

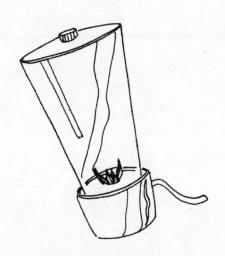

Chapter 14

Herbs and Spices

The following is a brief summary of the herbs and spices I have used in this book, plus a few extra items for interest and reference.

Agar-agar is a powder made from a tasteless sea algae, used as a jelling agent in place of animal gelatin. Not widely available, it can usually be obtained from good herbalists or Chinese stores, although in the latter it is often flavored with synthetic vanilla. Most health food stores carry it in powder or flake form.

Allspice resembles very large black peppercorns, but it is commonly sold in ground form. It is called allspice because the flavor is similar to a mixture of cinnamon, cloves, and nutmeg. Use it freshly ground in cakes and cookies and in sweet vegetable dishes based on squash, parsnip, or sweet potato. Try it also in curries, chutneys, and pickles.

Aniseed This licorice-tasting spice was used by the ancient Egyptians, Greeks, and Romans. It is good in bread and cakes, and improves the flavor of figs and hot chestnuts. It is widely used in vegetable dishes in India and China. Try it with bean dishes and in curries. The seeds, simmered for a few minutes in boiling water, make a very refreshing tea.

Arrowroot is a fine, easily digested starch made from the root of a tropical American plant. When made into a custard with milk, it helps settle stomach upsets and is good to take with fruit after a long fast.

Asafetida (Hing) The name means "stinking gum." I once threw out a friend's entire supply, believing it to be rotten garlic. Asafetida is derived from the sap of a relative of the fennel plant and was a favorite flavoring of the Romans, who called it silphium, but it is likely that the variety they used, said to be the best, came from a plant now extinct. Do not use it in anything that is not to be cooked, but otherwise use sparingly in savory dishes. It is not readily found on supermarket shelves, but can be obtained at a good health food store or from Indian or Middle Eastern stores.

Basil, Sweet Used fresh, basil is delicious in tomato salad with salt and olive oil, and as an ingredient in all tomato-based dishes. The fresh leaf is the essential ingredient of the Italian delicacy pesto. Also use fresh basil in all types of soups, stews, sauces, stuffings, pies, and dips. If you must go on a long journey, take a few leaves to brighten up the dismal food you will probably have to eat on the way. Once accustomed to fresh basil, you will never again be satisfied with the dried leaf. Fortunately, fresh basil can be preserved by packing the leaves into glass jars in between layers of salt and covering with olive oil. This will keep all through the winter, and retains the characteristic flavor, even though the leaves turn black.

Bay Leaf is the leaf of the Sweet Laurel or Sweet Bay Tree, usually sold whole and dried. Use in all savory dishes, and boil it in milk for custards, too. If you intend to blend recipes in a blender, take out the bay leaves first, as they will otherwise give the food a bitter flavor.

Capers are the buds of small flowers that grow wild around the Mediterranean. They are pickled in vinegar to obtain the characteristic flavor. Use in salads, and hot or cold sauces for an unusual sour but subtle effect. Also good on pizzas.

Caraway Seed Use caraway seeds sparingly in bread, cakes, and pastries. Try them in homemade cheese and sautéed cabbage. The young leaves of the plant can also be eaten if you can find them.

Cardamom This is a delicious Eastern spice, but beware of inferior closely related substitutes. The genuine cardamom pods are green or buff-colored and about the size of a pea, and the small black seeds are packed together inside. Open the pods to remove the seeds. Grind the seeds as you need them, and use in curries, cakes, pastries, and milk desserts. Also delicious in hot milk, spiced fruit punch, and fruit salads. Good for the digestion and sometimes chewed alone after meals.

Cayenne Pepper is made from a certain species of hot red chili peppers that originally grew in Cayenne in French Guyana. It is a little lighter in color and finer in texture than other types of chili powder, but the uses are identical (see below).

Chamomile is a yellow, daisy-like flower. Chamomile makes a soothing tea, good at bedtime and after long stressful journeys.

Chili Powder Ground from the small red chili pepper, chili powder is used whenever a hot effect is required, but it has little other flavor. Try to get pure chili powder, and beware of chili mixes, which usually contain garlic. Chili makes a nice change from black pepper, sprinkled sparingly on sandwiches.

Cinnamon is a sweet spice (from the bark of a tree) which is difficult to grind at home. Buy it freshly ground in small quantities and use it to flavor chutneys, drinks, cakes, cookies, fruit, breakfast cereals, and milk desserts. A little sprinkled with sugar on buttered toast is nice for breakfast. Try vanilla ice cream with cinnamon and nutmeg mixed in.

Cloves The flower bud of a small shrub-like tree native to the islands of southeast Asia and flourishing only near the sea. It is the most important export of Zanzibar. Buy whole and use sparingly, grinding as needed, for chutneys, cakes, cookies, curries, hot fruit punches, and especially apple pie.

Coriander/Cilantro Coriander is known as one of the most ancient and useful herbs, both for its aromatic leaves (also called cilantro) and for the seed, which has a warm, mild flavor delicious in soups, sauces and stews, as well as curries. All curry powder contains coriander seed as a major ingredient. As a spice it can be used liberally and is kind to the inexperienced cook. The leaves have a unique aroma and flavor that is indispensable for authentic Eastern and Mexican dishes.

Cumin is a small seed available from Indian stores where it is called jiira (pronounced "jeera"). Although an important curry spice, cumin has wider uses in many soups, stews, salads, sauces, pies, etc., wherever a primarily savory flavor is required. It is difficult to grind at home, so buy it freshly ground in small quantities. Try the whole seed in bread dough and homemade cheeses, spicy pancake batter, and curries.

Dill Fresh dill leaf is interesting in many recipes. Think of it for dishes involving sour cream, yogurt or cheese, potatoes, and cucumbers. Try a little in vegetable soups and salads. The leaf does not dry well, but can be frozen. The seed is also used, but is strong and bitter with a flavor similar to caraway, and has similar uses. It can ruin a vegetable dish if used as a substitute for the leaf.

Fennel is a vegetable, but the seeds are used as a spice, with a flavor similar to anise. Simmered in water, fennel seeds make a very refreshing tea which is good as a remedy for indigestion. Fennel seed is an ingredient in the Chinese 5-spice mix (anise, star-anise, cassia, fennel, and cloves) which is good with beans and vegetables in Chinese cooking. The seeds are a little too strongly flavored to be used regularly in vegetable dishes and should be used cautiously in culinary experiments.

Fenugreek A tiny orange bean, fenugreek is very easily sprouted to make a lovely spicy salad sprout which, like all sprouts, enlivens winter salads very inexpensively. Fenugreek also adds subtlety to spicy foods. Use whole or roast and grind. It is available from Indian stores, known as methi.

Galangal An oriental root with a flavor a little resembling a combination of white pepper and ginger, but milder and with its own distinct subtle taste and aroma. Look for galangal in Chinese specialty delis, where it may be available either as a dried root or a powder. It is delicious in gluten recipes, in tofu and buckwheat dishes, and in soups, stir-frys, and cold grain salads whenever a subtle, distinctively Oriental touch is desired.

Garam Masala The name means warm mixed spice. It is used for curries, but has a sweeter aroma than curry powder. It spices up sweet vegetables such as squash and parsnip in soups and pies.

Ginger was used as a medicine against plague in the dark days of the Black Death, because it promotes sweating. Fresh ginger is excellent grated and used in spicy dishes of beans, cooked vegetables, salads, and fruit salad. Dried powdered ginger is good in milky puddings, cookies and cakes and is the traditional seasoning for slices of melon. Crystallized ginger is the fresh root preserved in sugar, and is a delicacy eaten alone or sprinkled on the crust of ginger cake. Finally, stem ginger which is not really the stem of the plant but the young peeled root preserved in a sugar syrup, is good with ice cream, banana, and chocolate sauce. For a bad cold, try a hot mix of water with lemon, honey and a sprinkling of powdered ginger. Use the powder in hot fruit punch on cold nights, or in warm milk and honey at bedtime.

Lavender This lovely scented herb, combined with fennel seeds, makes a fragrant tea.

Lemon Verbena Use the leaves to make a fragrant, lemony tea.

Mace is a spice ground from the fronds surrounding nutmeg. It is nice in creamy soups and milk-based sauces, and similar to nutmeg, but more subtle. Always use sparingly.

Marjoram is an exceedingly useful herb with a warm flavor that is preserved well when the leaves are dried. It can be used whenever a fragrant, herbed effect is desired. The flavor is easily lost, so use marjoram towards the end of cooking soups and stews, or sauté it. It is also nice in salad dressings and bean dips. Like coriander, it is a great standby and friend to cooks with little experience as it won't ruin a dish if overdone.

Mint Use fresh mint in salad dressings, fruit salads, and in summer soups and sauces, and especially with pea and potato dishes. It is very easy to grow in a garden or window box, and dries easily if snipped and hung upside-down in bunches. You can then use it all winter as an herb and tea leaf.

Mustard This is an ancient spice used by the Greeks and Romans and mentioned in the Bible. The characteristic flavor is the result of a chemical reaction when the ground seed is mixed with cold water and left for 10-15 minutes. If the ground seed is mixed with vinegar this reaction will not occur, and the flavor will be less pungent and more bitter. Therefore, for the mustard taste, mix mustard with cold water and leave to stand before you use it in mayonnaise. Mustard oil is used in India for cooking, as are the whole (black) seeds. Recently, many new varieties of whole grain mustard mixes have become available in Europe and the United States, and it is fun to experiment with small quantities of these in your favorite recipes.

Nigella is a little black seed with a peppery aromatic flavor, sprinkled on breads and cakes in India and the Middle East. The French call it "quatre epices" (four spices). Try it in raitas and spicy breads, or sprinkle it over food as a change from pepper. Try also a little mixed with sesame seed to make gomasio (p. 143).

Nutmeg
Chaucer writes:

> *There springen herbs grate and smalle*
> *The licoris and the setewole*
> *And many a clove gilofre*
> *And note mege to put ale*
> *Whether it be moist or stale*

Nutmeg is lovely with spinach, Jerusalem artichokes, chestnuts and cheese dishes, as well as milk sweets such as rice pudding, and fruit punch. It has slightly soporific qualities and is good at bedtime in light warm drinks. It looks very pretty, too. Always freshly grind the whole nut.

Oregano is the classic pizza herb and the secret of an excellent pizza. Try it also in all other tomato dishes and with eggplant, zucchini, potatoes, spinach, pasta, cheese, and beans.

Paprika is a mild spice which is ground from a special variety of dried red bell peppers. It can be used liberally in goulash and creamy salad dips but goes well with almost anything savory. Another one for the cautious or inexperienced cook.

Parsley is indispensable for good cooking. It is the first food I can remember eating, at three years of age! It is very nutritious, rich in iron and vitamins A and C (but drink the fresh juice sparingly as large doses of vitamin A are toxic), and improves virtually any savory dish. Keep it as you would keep fresh flowers, standing in water rather than in the refrigerator. The stalks are the tastiest part and quite acceptable if finely chopped. The dried leaf is a miserable substitute, but fresh parsley is often available in good supermarkets all year round.

Pepper There are two basic varieties of ground pepper, black and white, prepared by processing the peppercorns in two different ways. Everybody has their preference for one or the other. The important thing is that it should be freshly ground, and for this it is worth buying a mill. If you mill your own pepper, you can also try other varieties of peppercorns.

Poppy Seeds These tiny black seeds are used as fillings and decoration for confectionery, and (after being hulled) to thicken curries in India where starchy flours are never used for this purpose. They have a pleasant nutty flavor when roasted and are also very decorative in pasta dishes.

Rosemary is a very strong cooking herb that goes well with root vegetables, dark greens, and celery in soups and stews, or sprinkled over oven roasted carrots, parsnips, and potatoes with coarse grain salt. Always use sparingly, especially in soup which will be blended, as too much will ruin a dish, giving it a bitter taste impossible to disguise.

Saffron is the dried stigma of the saffron crocus. There are just three stigmas in each crocus, and these must be hand-harvested. It takes up to a quarter of a million flowers, which represents a staggering amount of hand labor, to produce just one pound of saffron, which is why it is so expensive. However, a tiny pinch will give color and fragrance to a large dish. Use in rice-based recipes with cashews and raisins and similarly with millet, couscous, and bulgur wheat.

Sage is delicious with all beans and cheeses, and in lentil, nut, and carrot dishes baked or roasted in the oven. Use sparingly — it's hard to get just the right amount, but less is better than more.

Savory Though it is an herb similar in appearance to rosemary, the flavor of savory is very different. Useful with beans and in soups and stews, but use sparingly. Like rosemary, it is good sprinkled over oven-roast root vegetables.

Sorrel is a sour herb rich in iron. Use in lentil and tomato soups and in sour sauces for green vegetables.

Tamarind is from the bark of a tree. It produces a sour brown juice that gives an authentic flavor to Indian curries. It can be bought as a paste and keeps a long time.

Tarragon Authentic French tarragon is difficult to obtain as a fresh herb, even in France, where it is essential for a great many traditional recipes. The difficulty is that the true French tarragon rarely produces high-quality seeds, and propagation must be by cuttings or root division. Tarragon grown from seed almost always has an inferior flavor. Also, dried tarragon is a poor substitute for the fresh leaf. The best way to get the authentic tarragon flavor is to use tarragon vinegar which adds a subtle, delicious flavor to salads and marinades for stir-frys and tempuras. Use fresh tarragon in milk- or cream-based soups, sauces, stuffings, and to make tarragon butter. The fresh leaf freezes well.

Thyme There are many cultivated varieties of thyme, but serious cooks advocate gathering the wild herb fresh on a Mediterranean hillside. Fortunately, fresh thyme does dry well and is very useful for seasoning all savory dishes. Thyme is at its best when baked very slowly for a long time in oven casseroles. Like rosemary, it gives a lovely fragrance to vegetables roasted slowly in the oven.

Turmeric You will always have to buy this bright yellow powder freshly ground, so buy only small quantities. Use sparingly in curries and with dishes based on corn or potatoes. A little pinch added to rice and other grains gives a pleasant golden coloring and for added effect you can decorate the finished dish with paprika. A little turmeric in warm milk at bedtime is an alternative to nutmeg, cinnamon, or ginger. Turmeric is said to be good for keeping the joints supple.

Vanilla grows as the pod of an orchid about 6 inches long and dark brown or black in color. The pod sparkles when fresh, but the crystalline appearance is unfortunately easy to fake, so beware of old or poor-quality pods. The pods are obtainable ground to powder, marinated in alcohol to make extract, or used whole, in which case they are recyclable. Cook the pod with the food, then remove, wash, dry, and store again for re-use. Alternatively, store several pods in a jar of sugar, into which the flavor and aroma will diffuse. Use vanilla or vanilla sugar in all milk sweets, cakes, cookies, ice cream, and breakfast cereals.

NEW WORLD LIBRARY is dedicated to publishing books and cassettes that help improve the quality of our lives. If you enjoyed *Vegetarian Food for All*, we highly recommend the following books:

Granola Madness: The Ultimate Granola Cookbook by Katherine Dieter and Donna Wallstin. *Granola Madness* combines the culinary and literary credentials of authors Dieter and Wallstin. The result is a practical, witty, and inspiring primer on creating the kind of granola that's worth getting out of bed for.

The Vegetarian Lunchbasket by Linda Haynes. 225 easy, nutritious recipes for the quality-conscious family on the go! If you're stuck in a rut of packing peanut butter sandwiches every day, this book will pull you out of it — permanently! This is family food — hearty and unpretentious.

Cooking for Consciousness: Whole Food Recipes for the Vegetarian Kitchen by Joy McClure and Kendall Layne. A comprehensive and practical guide to the world of natural foods and nutrition, this is a basic "must-have" cookbook for the whole-foods kitchen of the '90s!

If you would like a catalog of our
fine books and cassettes, contact:

NEW WORLD LIBRARY
14 Pamaron Way
Novato, California 94949

(415) 884-2100 • Fax: (415) 884-2199
Or call toll-free: (800) 227-3900